THE COMMONER SYNDROME

▼

THE COMMONER SYNDROME

▼

Twenty-first Century Roadblock

Mark Meek

Writers Club Press

San Jose New York Lincoln Shanghai

The Commoner Syndrome
Twenty-first Century Roadblock

Writers Club Press
an imprint of iUniverse.com, Inc.

For information address:
iUniverse.com, Inc.
5220 S 16th, Ste. 200
Lincoln, NE 68512
www.iuniverse.com

ISBN: 0-595-16443-9

Printed in the United States of America

I would like to dedicate this book to immigrants. About 130 million people live in countries other than the one of their birth. No matter which country they came from or which country they are in now, I believe that anyone with the get-up-and-go to pack up and begin life in an entirely new land deserves to have a book dedicated to them.

INTRODUCTION

For generations after the industrial revolution, the lives of the commoners and elites of society revolved around farms or factories. Commoners had their modest homes and lives of labor with usually no widespread changes over the period of a lifetime. Capitalism arose and turned into the most efficient system.

By the end of the second world war, technical progress had neared a point of critical mass, and not just in the atomic bomb. The United States was the only advanced country not badly damaged by the war and a great explosion of knowledge and technical progress and along with it, a massive expansion of the economy became possible.

A number of promising new fields of technology had came about, among them were nuclear energy, rockets, computers and microwave communications. The United States became the focal point of the postwar world's technical and economic development. A great demand for labor created a large, suburban middle class. It seemed as if expansion could continue indefinitely if only enough brainpower and entrepreneurial energy was available.

As time went on, other advanced countries made a full recovery from the second world war and industrialism spread to the third world. Technical progress only made workers replaceable with automation. The door was closing on American laborers while another was opening, the never-ending need for professionals and other elite positions. The large middle class was not going to last forever and it hopefully was serving as a springboard for people to reach higher things by making it possible for workers to afford college tuitions or, put aside capital to start or expand businesses.

This is where difficulties appeared, education was easily available and opportunity was none too difficult to find. But this great expansion in technology and the economy was virtually unprecedented in history on such a scale and it had all happened so fast. We were still largely a nation of commoners from a cultural point of view. Being impeded in keeping up with economic and technical progress by people's commoner heritage is what I have named the commoner syndrome.

In the early 1990s, the U.S. government set down the goal that American children were to be number one in mathematics and science in the world by the year 2000. As of this writing, we have not come close to this goal but rather have slipped further. I am convinced that this goal is impossible until the commoner syndrome is fully understood.

The education community is trying everything to ensure that children will be ready for the future. Reforming the school system, getting back to core subjects, implementing basic competency exams for teachers as well as students are all ideas being considered. Apparently, the role of the commoner syndrome in holding things back is not receiving much attention. The reason for this book is to change that. If we are ever going to really reach for the stars, the commoner syndrome will have to be overcome.

CHAPTER ONE

---▼---

PYRAMIDS, PEAKS, PENDULUMS AND, PROGRESS

We all know that nature operates by a food pyramid. On the bottom are the plants and the trillions of microscopic creatures that provide food for somewhat larger living things. As we go higher on the pyramid, animals tend to get both larger and fewer in number. The natural predator and prey relationship can be found in any ecosystem.

This pyramid structure is visible virtually anywhere there is a system of some kind with some components larger than others. In the universe when stars are forming, there tends to be many smaller stars born for each larger one.

The pyramid structure is also primal to human organizations. As a whole, there is always fewer bosses than workers, fewer officers than soldiers, fewer teachers than

students, fewer chiefs than subjects and, fewer professionals than common laborers. With the fewer in each case
occupying the limited space in the upper reaches of the
pyramid, while the many fill the vast lower area of the fig-
urative pyramid. The different levels work together, the
pyramid-shaped system could not function otherwise.

We could make a general division of the human pyramid into "elite" and "commoner". Everyone is a part of a
number of different pyramids at once. By age, the few eld-
ers are at the top, the many youngsters at the bottom. By
nation, the few rich superpowers at the top, the many
poor countries at the bottom. But, the elite/commoner
division concerns an individual's permanent role in society
and has been prominent all through history, all across the
world.

HISTORY OF THE HUMAN PYRAMID

To review how we got to where we are today, let's go
back to the last millenium change, the year 1000. The
Viking raids in northern Europe were pretty much past.
But warfare among powerful families was not. There was
also the threat of raiding Moslems and Huns in certain
areas. The continuous inter-family fighting created a
requirement for two separate social classes. One was an
elite of highly trained warriors, the other was the numerous peasants, who the warriors protected and who kept the
warriors supplied.

This was the beginning of the social order known as
"feudalism". It developed differently in different regions. It
is associated mainly with the middle ages but it lasted

longer in some areas. In parts of eastern Europe, it was still to be found in the twentieth century.

Middle ages nobles would give others use of their land in return for military and other services. The parcel of land was known as a "feud" or "fief", giving feudalism it's name. Some small landowners sought protection from powerful neighbors. The neighbors gave military assistance in return for agricultural products. Big landowners requesting military assistance paid for it by giving some of their land to knights.

A boy of noble blood began training as a knight at age seven in a lord's castle. He did various chores and learned the correct manners. At sixteen, he became a squire and followed the lord into battle or on hunting trips. When the lord thought him ready, he was knighted.

Most farms in the middle ages were large manors owned by a lord. Most farmers were tenants on these manors. The lord lived in a fortified manor house or castle. The tenant's cottages formed a village near the manor or castle. Beyond the village, fields were marked off. Some of the land was reserved for the lord. Each family had a private garden. The entire domain was an independent community.

All feudal systems considered the king as the owner of all land. He gave estates known as "fiefs" to vassals. These could be nobles who inherited their estates, or those receiving land in return for a number of warriors. Vassals who were dukes, counts or, abbots probably had vassals of their own. In the lower reaches of society's pyramid as we might expect, were the multitude of peasants.

There were two kinds of peasants; freemen and serfs. Freemen often obtained their land in return for military service. Serfs came with the land as did their children although, the lord could not sell them. Serfs made up the vast majority of Europe's population by far.

Many towns grew up around castles and forts during the middle ages. Towns could gain their freedom from the lord by military service or payment. When this happened, the town was given a "charter" signed by the lord. Business revolved around the central market which most towns had. The first merchant and craft guilds formed around this time.

A master of a craft would hire an apprentice, who was declared a journeyman to the guild when he had learned his trade. The journeyman would work for other masters to learn still more about the craft. When the journeyman had enough knowledge and experience, he could apply to the guild to be declared a master by displaying a "master-piece" he had made.

The middle ages are best known for the crusades, the series of attempts to capture the holy land. Many serfs earned their freedom by military service. It opened the eyes of Europeans to the outside world. Ships returning to Venice, Genoa and, Pisa brought such previously unseen items as ivory, jewels, spices and, fine silks. This did much to bring about the age of discovery two hundred years later, resulting in settlement of the new world.

In the early 1700's, Europe's town and city populations were growing. But most Europeans still produced their own food in small communities as they had during the middle ages. Most rural communities were self-sufficient for essentials. Besides farming, village craftsmen made the few necessities that a family might not have time or knowledge to make for itself. Luxuries were scarce.

In the countryside, many families earned extra money by such things as embroidery and weaving. Some craftsmen employed two or three apprentices. These "cottage industries" were of course, limited by the cost of transportation along with bad roads. Without good transport, a craftsman could not sell his products to a wide area. Which did not matter anyway because without better machinery, he could not increase his output and afford to hire more laborers.

Among the larger enterprises of the time, most of the work was still done in the employees' homes. This was sometimes called the "putting out" system. But soon, large factory buildings would be necessary.

In the mid-1700's, a marvelous machine was invented known as the steam engine. Coke, made from coal was found to be better and less expensive for iron smelting than charcoal. The steam engine launched a series of new inventions. This was to be known as the industrial revolution. A few areas such as Britain and the Ruhr valley in Germany were fortunate to have both iron ore and coal and joined the industrial revolution early.

Machinery made of iron and powered by steam made for cheap and abundant manufactured goods.

Industry expanded rapidly, starting in Britain. The new machines of the industrial revolution were much too big to fit in the workers' homes as in the cottage industries. Factories appeared all over the landscape to house them. The factories became the hubs of new towns because workers had to live near them. The industrial revolution was unstoppable, even though not everyone wanted to adapt to it. One group in Britain, the Luddites, actually tried to reverse the industrial revolution by sabotaging the machines.

By 1900, industry had overtaken agriculture in economic importance in the world. Millions of people lived in large industrial cities. Canals, roads, railroads and, steamships went anywhere that was necessary to meet the needs of industry. The network of communications needed in a world dominated by industry had seeded yet another revolution just as momentous as the industrial revolution. Farming was improved to feed the armies of factory workers.

Many industrialists were made rich by the expanding industry along with merchants by the resulting trade, joining the landowning upper class with it's political power and prestige. Factory workers were crowded together in hastily-built unhealthy cities and tried to cooperate to improve their lot and meager wages. The political and social movements that were to shape modern society emerged.

Medical advances and agricultural improvements produced some unexpected consequences. Europe's population exploded around this time. Anyone who wanted to farm instead of work in a factory as in past generations or who could not find work, or who simply longed for wide open spaces and a chance to better themselves had an option. The new world, first colonized several hundred years before, was now a modern society as Europe was. It had more space than Europe but much less people. There was room and work for the excess millions of Europe who wanted to come as immigrants. And the steam engines that powered the industrial revolution made possible the large, fast ships needed to carry these immigrants across the ocean. (Did God plan it that way?)

PEAKS

Aside from the pyramid, another pattern seen when dealing with living things is the peak. In contrast with non-living things, living things tend to have optimum requirements. This means that anything involving living beings has a certain amount called the optimum or ideal which any amount either less or greater would not be as beneficial or desirable. If displayed on a graph, a peak would show at the optimum point, which any other point on the graph would be below. Since human beings are the most complex creatures, we would naturally expect them to have an optimum point or peak for many different aspects of their existence.

We, or any other creature has a temperature at which we feel and function best. We can be too cold or too warm or, just right. When we eat, having too little or too much is not as satisfactory as having just the right amount. Too much work and not enough play, or vice versa is detrimental. There is a point, or peak that is ideal. Even having everything too ideal with no stress is detrimental, again there is a peak of stress such as exercise and discipline that is just right. Doing a scientific analysis of a living being would involve many peak factors.

In contrast, non-living matter lacks the peak factor. An inorganic chemical reaction proceeds faster with more heat. There is no point at which it peaks; the hotter, the better. A forest fire does not have an optimum amount of wood; simply, the more, the better. A star in the formation process does not have a peak amount of hydrogen for best results; the more, the better.

Related to the concept of peaks is the shape known in statistics as the bell curve. That is a few of any given component formed naturally will tend to be at the top of a given category, a few will chance to be at the bottom and the vast majority will be in the middle between them. The graphical shape known as the bell curve. This bell curve is so-called because it is usually shaped like a bell. It usually fits students' grades, people's height or weight and many other factors occuring randomly. A few people are exceptionally tall, a few very short but, the majority in between near the average. Usually, the more samples are taken, the more accurate a picture is displayed and the more the curve looks like a bell. The bell curve is probably used most to portray the middle class. A few wealthy people, a few poor and the majority middle class in between.

Those people who run industry, business and, agriculture are especially interested in the peak concept in the way their operations are running. They naturally want the most and best productivity for the least initial expenditure. This would form a peak on a graph as the maximum profit. In a business situation in a large market, such as those that formed as the industrial revolution advanced and spread and the population grew rapidly, it is not as simple to tell where the peak is as it is in such a simple situation as deciding if you are too hot or too cold. In such a case, the only sure way to achieve maximum profits is to use a pendulum to find the peak.

PENDULUMS

A pendulum is a vital pattern in the workings of our economic system just as the pyramid pattern is vital to the structure of nature and human society. The pendulum is just as important in nature as the pyramid, to manage the relationship between different levels of nature's pyramid. When nature uses the pendulum pattern to find a peak, it keeps the different levels of the food pyramid in balance.

Just as the pyramid pattern can be used to describe both the food chain in nature and the typical structure of human organizations, the pendulum pattern has applications both in nature and in human economic activity.

In the food chain pyramid, all relationships between predator on one level and prey on a higher level are managed by a pendulum that swings one way and then the other until the peak of harmony is found. When the population of rabbits climbs above the norm, it means that there is more food available for coyotes and their population is able to increase. The many coyotes hunting for dinner and to feed their pups drastically reduces the number of rabbits around. Meaning that the particular area will not be able to feed so many coyotes, reducing their population. Meaning that rabbits, who eat only plants, have more freedom to multiply without being hunted and their numbers increase. Meaning that the coyotes can increase, and so on. A never-ending pendulum always seeking a peak of harmony between the levels of the food pyramid.

Nature rewards those creatures that adapt successfully and, since there is never enough food for every creature that does or could exist, it eliminates those who do not adapt to favor those that do. The natural balance of things

is sometimes thrown out of balance by some kind of catastrophe, but the pendulum eventually finds it's former
position.

Few people in the world today doubt that capitalism is
the most efficient economic system.

Have you ever wondered why? Simply because it works
on the same principle that nature has been working on for
millions of years. Capitalism is sometimes called "free
enterprise" meaning that anyone who sees a way to make
money can go into business and do so as long as they have
or can get the "capital" to get started.

The economy could not support as many people as
there are who would like to start or expand a business. So,
it works like nature does, a business has to show a profit or
it does not make sense for it's owner to keep it open so, it
closes and makes room for those that are making a profit.
The business has to produce the best possible product and
provide the best possible service at the lowest possible
price in order to compete with similar businesses. The
ones who gain are the consumers and the system as a
whole because everything must be constantly improved to
stay in the game. Free enterprise is the most productive
system because it permits the maximum number of people
to work for themselves, and most people will work harder
for themselves than they will laboring for someone else.

Capitalism operates on the pendulum principle of supply and demand. When a product or service is scarce, in
other words the demand exceeds supply, it's providers are
able to charge more money for it. When it is abundant, or
supply exceeds demand, the market will not bear a high
price for it.

People who do not operate their own business in a capitalist economy sell their labor to earn a living. The wages a worker with a particular skill is able to earn also operate on the pendulum of supply and demand. Too few workers will earn more money each than too many workers.

Market forces will tell a businessman what to do to earn the peak of maximum possible profit. For example, the distance between the production site and consumption site determine transportation costs, which is effectively a part of production costs. Would it mean less expenditure in the long run to build a new factory nearer to the consumption site? Would an investment in the production facilities improve the product enough to justify higher prices on the market for it which would return a profit over the initial investment?

The capitalist pendulum also has a supply and demand factor for where people live. A capitalist laborer is expected to be a mobile labor seeker. But when more people want to live and seek work in an area than there is houses being built, houses get more expensive, eventually to the point that it dissuades people from living there. When many people leave an area, housing prices drop because of the lack of demand compared to supply. But if they drop low enough, people unable to afford a house in more expensive areas will move in. But at the same time, Builders want to build houses in those areas where there is maximum profit to be made. It amounts to a never-ending pendulum similar to that which has always kept nature in balance.

A capitalist system works on simple principles, yet we can go into great depth in analyzing it. The system can also be compared with the human body. When the body needs food, water, sleep or, is too hot or cold, or wants to go to the bathroom, it tells us. We can ignore it for a while, but not for long. It also operates on a pendulum pattern. Health, illness and, lifestyle forms another pendulum, an unhealthy lifestyle tends to swing the pendulum toward illness, hopefully a reverse swing of the pendulum brings the body back toward health.

A capitalist economy can also get very complex. Some companies sell shares of themselves to raise capital, called stocks. Stocks are bought, sold and, traded in large markets called stock exchanges. Sometimes, there is a lot of trading and prices get high and many traders decide to stop buying at the same time. Prices that traders are willing to pay drop and so does the price of the stock. Since no one wants to buy a stock when it's worth is still falling, it drops still further. In extreme cases, this is known as a stock market crash. Prices were driven artificially high and the natural pendulum over-corrected and drove the prices artificially low.

Since capitalism is a pendulum, it works in cycles. Business activity builds to a peak and then drops because people only have so much money that they are willing to spend. Then, as prices go down too, activity builds back up again.

People do not usually barter goods and services, we use money issued by the government to represent the goods and services. The pendulum works here too, when the supply of money in circulation increases relative to the goods and services circulating in the economy, the relative value of each unit of money decreases, Prices increase to compensate and we have what is known as "inflation". The reverse situation is called deflation.

When people want to borrow money, it becomes a commodity in itself. During times of booming business activity, more people want to borrow money to use as capital and lending institutions can charge higher interest rates, which they could not when activity slows down.

Capitalism does have some basic requirements. Society must be fairly advanced, basic needs like food, clothing and, shelter must have been met. There must be a large enough market, requiring adequate transportation to go beyond the immediate community. It is not morally acceptable to make a profit from starving or homeless people or, in emergency situations. This is why real capitalism only arrived after the industrial revolution.

Capitalism also has another important requirement to function. A system of government in harmony with the principles of capitalism. The form of government that almost always accompanies capitalism is known as democracy. The familiar pyramid structure is easily visible in a democracy, president or prime minister at the peak, on down through state or provincial and, county governments to mayors and city councils with the voters spread out equally at the base of the pyramid.

The pendulum pattern also is as much a part of democracy as of capitalism, although often over a longer term. There are usually two main parties in most democracies but there may be more. It is a mirror of capitalism. Each party promises that all kinds of wonderful things will happen if only the people will vote them and their candidate into office. The party that is out of power points out how miserably the one in power is failing to keep it's promises and that the expected wonderful things will not happen until they are elected. It is up to the voters to decide. As in capitalism, political parties must achieve the best possible results to compete with the opposing party and must advertise their capabilities as companies must advertise their products. Capitalism is a mirror of democracy in that consumers "vote" every time they choose one product over a competing product, while manufacturers vie to have the best product. Successful companies are "elected "to remain, while the others go out of business.

In practice, the country tends to benefit from both parties and their ideas and the pendulum usually swings from one side to the other. In the United States since world war two for example, the Democrats with FDR and Truman were followed by the Republicans with Eisenhower. Which was followed by the Democrats with Kennedy and Johnson. Which was followed by the Republicans with Nixon and Ford. Which was followed by the Democrats with Carter. Which was followed by the Republicans with Reagan and Bush. Which was followed by the Democrats with Clinton. A predictable, long-term pendulum.

Capitalism works together with democracy. Like every other aspect of the system, this relationship is static rather than dynamic. The interplay between capitalism and democracy also follows the pendulum pattern. When the interests of capitalist business comes first, it is said that the system leans to the right. This side is called the Republican, Conservative or, Tory in various countries. When the interests of the majority of voters, which are laborers, comes first, it is said that the system leans to the left. This side is called the Democrat or, Labour in various countries.

There is some conflict between those near the top in a democracy and those near the bottom. It is not that they are not going to work together, but just how they are going to work together. It is generally believed that the right generates more wealth but the left distributes the wealth more evenly. That business is concerned most with short-term profit and government with long-term policy. Maybe society needs a little of both, which is where the pendulum comes in.

A company must have it's own mini-government, starting with the owner or owners at the top. If the company is publicly owned through it's stock, this is elected through a limited democratic process through the board of directors. The pendulum pattern usually shows up here too in large, long-lasting corporations. In an auto manufacturer for example, CEO's tend to follow the pattern of one from the financial side of the operation, followed by one from the engineering side, followed by another from the financial side, and so on.

This interplay upon which capitalism operates is fundamental to all human interactions. Which is of course, why capitalism is the most efficient system. The desire to be liked, the attraction to the opposite sex and the search for a suitable mate all have an interplay fitting the same pattern as capitalism. We usually have to invest in being nice to other people because it is profitable for them to be nice to us. Achieving success in the capitalist economy helps bring success in finding a good mate. We refrain from being rude to people, at least some of the time, because we compare it to it's cost of having them be rude to us in return. We refrain from the luxury of firing missiles at countries that we disapprove of, again at least some of the time, in order not to have to pay the price of missiles launched at us.

PROGRESS

Capitalism as we know it today began after the industrial revolution. It was productive, but was not necessarily the best system for all the people. It took a dynamic interplay between the old capitalism, democracy, socialism and, communism to get the efficient and livable system that we have today.

Around 1900, the western countries were in the gilded age of capitalism. If you happened to be a J.P. Morgan, a Rockefeller or, a Rothschild, you pretty much had it made. But if you were not, chances are that you would be spending a life of squalor putting in long, backbreaking days in the factory or field of someone a lot better off than you.

The industrial revolution had made the feudalism of the middle ages obsolete. Capitalism would not have been workable under feudalism. But the factories and mills that began to dot the landscape were owned by the elite who could afford them, who got richer still on the work of the common laborers. Forming society into clear-cut economic classes who inevitably socialized and intermarried almost exclusively with members of the same class. Virtually everyone was effectively locked into the class of their birth. Feudalism had simply been replaced by an economic and social class system. Is it any wonder that stories like "Treasure Island" and "Robin Hood", who stole from the rich to give to the poor never lost their popularity.

The grievances set down by Karl Marx, a German Jew who spent most of his life in exile in England and, France, had a tremendous amount of justification. Since the industrial revolution, Capitalism had run wild. Being an everyday laborer under raw capitalism is not much of a life and, communism, based on the theories of Marx, gained many followers.

Capitalism was full of flaws that only made communism more attractive in many quarters. The devastating stock market crash of 1929 was the low point of capitalism and the best possible advertisement for communism, which had started it's world revolution against the injustices of capitalism with Russia and Mongolia by this time. However, we can now see that if any cure was ever worse than the disease it was intended to cure, it is communism.

If the western countries were to be real democracies, the capitalist system had to be improved in the interests of the great majority instead of just the elite few. But at least capitalism operated by natural rythms, as we have seen.

Communists tried to artificially fix wages and prices. It told people where to live and usually which job to take. The system was supposed to represent the common worker, the proletariat, the hammer and sickle stood for industry and agriculture. But they could not vote in a real way and their views were ignored in favor of the "wisdom" of communist party officials.

Socialism is not capitalism free to run wild, or "laissez-faire" capitalism. It was not communism, although it was concerned for the common people and not just the elite. It is basically a capitalist, free enterprise economy in which the usually democratic government takes an active role, not just setting policies but in owning and operating certain sectors of the economy. Obviously, socialism can exist over a wide range. What happened is that capitalism adopted some of the principles of socialism without altering it's basic nature. Socialist ideas such as improved working conditions and education for the majority of the people, free or easily available health care for everyone, minimum wage and maximum working hours laws made a happier and, healthier society with opportunity for everyone. Communism, which was capitalism's competitor lost much of it's appeal.

Capitalism, working with democracy is a game. But we want the game to keep going, not for a few people to get all the marbles at the expense of everyone else. Democracy has term limits imposed. Capitalism has anti-trust laws. Everyone has to obey the same legal system. No one man is allowed to gain too much power. Private monopolies are prevented. The basic fault of capitalism is that it works in cycles, a rise followed by a fall. The democratic government that works along with the capitalist system tries by various methods to smooth out these natural cycles of capitalism.

Probably everyone has some kind of interest not only in succeeding but in helping the world along. Combined with the profit motive, this is why we do not still live in caves. Free enterprise capitalism which allows anyone to make the most use of their talents and uses natural competition to force continuous improvement of products and services, has proven to be the best at bringing that about. The observation that necessity is the mother of invention also fits with capitalism. Capitalist cosumers want the latest technologies and industries need it to keep up. The gilded age of capitalism could not have lasted, as technology advanced and the economy expanded, the enterprise and brainpower of far more people than just the few elites with control of the system was needed. Even when the system shows flaws, it is adaptable and flexible and works along with democracy to rectify things.

Capitalism was the ideological engine driving the creation of wealth. But capitalism left to run wild will do nothing but create a miserable life for everyone but the few with most of the riches. It was, at the time, out of harmony with the democracy with which it functions. However, one of capitalism's great strengths is adaptability and it adopted some of socialism's principles to become the most efficient system today with no doubt.

We saw how capitalism can be compared to the human body. Socialism is to a certain extent, a mild version of communism. And just as a doctor would give you a mild form of a contagious disease to act as a vaccination, to enable your body to develop resistance to the full disease, socialism acted as good medicine to capitalism, correcting the extremes that led to communism in the first place and vaccinating it against the cure that turned out to be worse than the disease.

You do not need to be an ecomonist to understand the commoner syndrome any more than you need to be an electrical engineer to change the batteries in a flashlight. It is just a little helpful to have a background review on how the system works and how we got where we are today.

CHAPTER TWO

▼

ELITE AND COMMONER TODAY

The old division of the human pyramid into elite and commoner is still very prevalent today. The major difference is that now, the division is not as sharp as in the days of feudalism or during the progress of industrialization. There is still the elite—commoner division but today in the developed countries, it is less a black and white, either -or, issue than one containing many shades of gray. There are really a whole spectrum of classifications in which we could place positions from commoner up to elite.

Most large enterprises have a sliding division of commoner and elite. In a factory, the highest level of management, accounting and, engineering would be considered elites. Any middle management levels would be lower if it were where a significant number of individuals spent their entire careers, less so if it were primarily a learning stage and a stepping stone to a higher level. Laborers, drivers, secretaries, security guards and, clerks would be the commoners. Foremen, tradesmen, computer operators and, technicians would often be a somewhat higher level of commoner. Any lower levels of management and such categories as computer programmers would be the next highest level.

Terms used to describe categories of workers are not as useful today as they were in the past to separate commoner from elite. The word "peasant" is little used today in the developed countries. Traditionally, a peasant was rural, working in agriculture while a commoner was urban, working in tasks other than farming. The terms "white collar" and, "blue collar" are often used. Although it does define the work environment, the terms are very general and are not congruent with the terms "elite "and" commoner".

Then we have the professions that fall somewhere in between. Is a first-class auto mechanic really a commoner because he gets dirty? He requires considerable knowledge but does that make him a full-fledged elite? Complicating things further are that there are elites among commoners and commoners among elites. In a gathering of strictly commoners, the elites would be the technicians, tradesmen, and in the military, sergeants. Also, in a gathering of elites, a few with stellar careers would stand out among the "common" elites.

There is no exact definition today as to what is a commoner and what is an elite that would fit every situation. But there are several criteria. Any task requiring a vast amount of knowledge taking a lengthy period to acquire relative to others would probably be considered as elite. As technology ever advances, the nearer to the cutting edge the profession, the more elite. Operating a small business involving no out of the ordinary technology would not be elite but, one involving a high level of technology would.

Volume is also a criteria, it is debatable if it is less so than technology. Owning and operating one small store may not be considered an elite task but with several such stores or one very large one, it may. Replacibility is perhaps the most important criteria overall. According to the capitalist law of supply and demand, someone easily replaced is a commoner, someone not easily replaced is an elite.

The most accurate definition of what differentiates elite from commoner today is the role that the individual plays in the economic world. Almost all blue collar workers would probably be considered as commoners as would many white collar workers. Professionals and higher-level management are usually considered as elite. The most questionable categories are sports, entertainment and, acting. The very little role that most of the participants actually play in running the world is offset by the very high visibility and earnings of the stars in these categories. We could safely say that any famous person, unless their fame is fleeting, is an elite.

For the purpose of understanding the commoner syndrome, it is not really necessary to define where exactly the division between commoner and elite is today if it even exists in any meaningful form.

When you drive west across the United States such as on Interstate 70, where would you say the dividing line between east and west is? A convenient point would seem to be when crossing the Mississippi river at St. Louis, where the arch was built as the "gateway to the west". But you may disagree, the grass and trees in Missouri look very "eastern", it is not until you enter Kansas that the terrain looks different from the rural eastern United States and seems "western". Maybe Kansas City instead of St. Louis should be considered as the gateway to the west.

But on the other hand, as long as you are heading in the direction you want to go, how much difference does it really make exactly where the dividing line is even if there is one? It is the same way with commoner and elite.

The definition of commoner and elite is flexible and changing. It certainly fluctuates by time and region. According to the capitalist laws of supply and demand, the more people of a certain profession there are in an area relative to demand, the less value each of their labor will be and the easier they will be to replace. In other words, they would each be more in the commoner direction than if there were fewer of them and more demand. It naturally follows that the people of the same profession would find themselves more to the elite side during boom times and more to the commoner side during a recession. In some areas of the country, there is a glut of grade school teachers, which in other circumstances would make the elite cut.

If we do not put any kind of age limit on when we define a person's role in the economic world as elite or commoner, that a student who will be an elite someday is in effect an elite right now undergoing training, then everyone, when young, is at least a semi-elite because their future is still open.

There is very obviously a difference between these two basic divisions of the human pyramid, various social ideas pretending that everyone's role in economic society is equal have only had a detrimental result. The traditional roles of elite and commoner have blurred in the twentieth century so that there is no neat dividing space, if one at all, but the roles are still existant.

DIFFERENCES BETWEEN COMMONER AND ELITE

Obviously, commoners and elites occupy different roles. But, what are the different characteristics that cause commoner and elite to be divided into different roles in the economy and different areas of the human pyramid?

There are many traditional images of the person as a commoner as opposed to an elite. But they tend to be simplistic and deceptive. Times are not as simple anymore and the images are often outdated.

The first deception is money. As you might expect, elites usually have more of it than commoners. But money is only one of the criteria used to separate commoner from elite. Today, like never before, a commoner may find his way into riches. Sudden riches do not make a commoner into an elite, although it can serve as capital or tuition to give the commoner a chance to pursue ambitions.

Similarly, an elite is naturally more likely than a commoner to have a college degree. But once again, some commoners have them and, a surprising number of elites do not. It is very true that generally elites are better educated and informed than commoners. There are sure to be a few exceptions but, the major difference is the use of this knowledge. A far greater portion of the elite's high-level knowledge is considered immediately or potentially useful. While the high-level knowledge posessed by a commoner is just for conversation or enlightenment.

Possibly the most important criteria for dividing elite from commoner, aside from role and replacibility in the economic world is the proximity to the cutting edge of technology. It is always elites that advance the world.

THE MILITARY

The military is very interesting to anyone concerned with commoners, elites and socio-economic classes. It is even more interesting today that the sharply defined gap between the top and bottom of the human pyramid of days past can now be described as blurred or even non-existant.

It is so interesting to us because the military is the place that makes the division between elite and commoner most obvious. Rules differ in various countries. But in all of them, the military is a modern mirror of many past strictly stratified societies. It is, in almost any country, an organization placing great importance on it's own history and traditions, not unlike some kind of exclusive brotherhood. Not only are the military escapades of the nation as a whole celebrated, but each branch and many individual units have the strong sense of history and tradition. Each branch of the military services wears a uniform unlike any other, which makes clearly visible everyone's rank and honors achieved. It may use weapons on the cutting edge of technology, but the military services are a reflection out of the past in terms of organization.

The most important aspect of the military in terms of understanding commoners and elites is obvious, it is organized much more like societies in centuries past than society today in that the officers, the elites, are a separate level altogether than the commoners, the NCO's and lower ranks. In America and other countries, separation of the two parts of the organizational pyramid is enforced to the point that socializing or "fraternizing" is forbidden or strongly discouraged. This is done to maintain the effectiveness of the chain of command but for our purpose, it illuminates the division between the levels of the human pyramid as it was in times past.

Interestingly, since civilian and military are opposite, just as elite and commoner are opposite, in traditional warfare, the common soldiers found themselves fighting and dying at the battlefront while the most valuable of the elites ran the war from a more secure location. In contrast, in the civilian world, the elites are at the cutting edge, the front , while the commoners are providing support behind the lines. In this respect, the army, which has been around since ancient times, is the most commoner of the services. The air force, which is the newest of the services, is the most elite and resembles civilian life more closely because there, it is the elite officer pilots that are on the cutting edge while the lower ranks provide support on the ground, behind the lines.

IT'S THE ROLE THAT COUNTS

The difference between elite and commoner is the role that is played in the world. This role is not personal, it is economic. It has nothing to do with personality or how outgoing a person is. It is not a matter of confidence. No positive thinking alone will make a commoner into an elite. Loss of confidence will not by itself make an elite into a commoner. An adult may or may not have self-confidence, a child may or may not have self-confidence, but the two are different beings although there is a connection between them.

It is a matter of the person's learned role in the world. Young lieutenants in the military may ask the advice of senior sergeants but nevertheless, one is still an elite and the other is a commoner.

In my opinion, it is ironically the commoner army's recruiting slogan "Be all that you can be" that best sums up what it is to be an elite.

ELITE IS BETTER

If elites are more important to society than commoners then it should show up in a better life for the elite, a kind of supply and demand factor, and it does. It is better for an individual to be an elite and better for a society to have more elites. Respect for elites has been a tradition down through history. Democracy says that all citizens are equal but capitalism says otherwise. From a capitalist point of view, it is vital for young commoners to see elites as models of achievement.

The one thing that an elite has that a commoner simply does not is the knowledge of being all you can be as far as your possible role in the world goes. In a society full of opportunities, does it not make a person into a little bit of a loser not to succeed? The world of an elite is largely open, that of a commoner is at least somewhat limited and closed. Elites must take care to choose the right profession but they have a much greater leeway in their careers, you will frequently see trained engineers and accountants working as managers and politicians.

Elites may work at commoner jobs when young and may be proud of it and learn a lot from it. When Peter the Great was czar of Russia and decided to modernize his country, he actually moved to the Netherlands and got a job in a shipyard as a laborer to learn how to best go about it. When Lyndon B. Johnson met with Alexei Kosygin, probably the two then most important elites in the world, each wore his commoner background like a badge. Johnson recalled his days of chopping cotton while Kosygin emphasized that he had actually done physical labor in a factory. But it is usually only for knowledge or to work one's way through college.

However, the fact is that since a commoner is not fulfilling his earthly potential, the human race as a whole is not fulfilling it's earthly potential. What advancements and solutions might the world find if it had say, twice the amount of working brainpower that it has now? We can only speculate but, the only way to achieve that is to turn a huge number of commoners into elites.

I have heard a theory that we, as individuals, use only ten or fifteen percent of our total brainpower or, something like that. I do not know how true it is or how we go about accessing the rest. I tend to think that the more we use our brains, the better we get at using them. But, I do know that the human race as a whole uses only a small fraction of it's total brainpower and skill potential, simply by having only a tiny fraction of the people doing tasks involving a great amount of knowledge and skill.

Look at America's path from a humble wilderness colony declaring it's independence in 1776 to the top of the world today. What do you suppose brought this about? What has America always been all about? About succeeding and becomong an elite, whatever an elite may be at any particular place and time.

As people achieve some of their ambitions and move up, America attracts other people who would like to be elites but cannot do it in their homelands. These immigrants or their children in turn also move up and make room for others. It was inevitable that America as a whole would rise up along with them. The world's most prosperous societies are those in which a commoner wants to be an elite and sees that it can be done with enough work and study without moving to another place, millions of such ambitious commoners pull the whole society up with them.

One vital ingredient is that upward mobility toward becoming an elite be a part of the culture. If enough people do not have the ambition to achieve a higher level, none of this will happen. America has always romanticized the ideal man and presidential candidate as a self-made rags to riches story. The poor boy makes good stories of Horatio Alger were very popular in the early twentieth century just as it was becoming possible for others besides the few at the top during the gilded age of capitalism to dream of being elites.

In a multi-ethnic and multi-racial society like America, much of the progress of all kinds of minorities in the twentieth century was probably due more to the expansion of elitism than we might think. Commoners tend to be more likely to be prejudiced than elites because they do not have the need to understand foreigners and ethnic minorities that elites do. Elites naturally look upon minorities and foreign nations as a potential market or, a source of materials or labor, or at least a source of useful knowledge.

While a commoner sees no need for such considerations. To him ambitious immigrants and foreigners willing to work for a dollar a day are only a threat to his livelihood. Also a commoner can compensate his position below the elites by prejudice against those that are different. I may be just a commoner, but at least I'm American, white, British, etc. When people are upwardly mobile they often forget about the prejudice that comes in handy as a scapegoat in less prosperous times.

Girls as students and women as workers will fare much better under an elite mentality than commoner for the same reasons. To the elite women in the workplace are a source of brainpower and labor, and their earnings from their jobs make them consumers. To commoners, women in the workplace are traditionally considered as taking a job away from a man.

No group benefits more from the move toward elitism and the advance of technology it brings than the physically handicapped. Think about the physically difficult typical commoner tasks. A physically handicapped person is simply shut out of the market. The brainpower they have is inaccessible to society. But the advance of society has changed that and all kinds of accessories are on the market for computers and other high technology to change that.

Commoners live in much more of a zero-sum game than elites. Simply because there are far fewer niches in the economy for commoners than elites. Elites have the power to create society. If unemployed, an elite has more of a chance to create his own position. There is not the need for resentments and jealousies among elites. Unlike commoners in their fixed positions, to an elite a person with a success story is someone to learn from. Elites and the upwardly mobile are free to achieve and create a life for themselves.

People are only human at all levels and some elites are known for their egos. But commoners have traditionally been known for their lack of positivity, which of course drains it out of those who do have it. If a commoner's station in life is relatively fixed, what reason is there for ambition and positivity? Keep in mind that this book is only about the role in the world, not about religion or, family.

Commonerism at it's worst has been known for it's lousy mediocrity, people with little good to say about each other, resenting those who do succeed. Unlike the elite with a real role in running the world, the commoner is likely to be preoccupied with trivial things.

A commoner has much more chance of going to prison than an elite and money is far from the only factor. Violence is much more a part of commoner culture than elite. A commoner is more likely to try to be a "tough guy" in order to compensate for his lower position, and this sometimes translates into violence. But the elites know that it is the brain that drives things.

Respect for elites is a tradition throughout human history, even in a democracy where everyone is supposedly equal. And this is justified, it is the elites that create society even though it is the commoners who do the labor.

CHAPTER THREE

▼

PROGRESS

Before going any further in our examination of commoners and elites, we should spend a couple of chapters examining the technical progress that has been made. A certain amount of progress was necessary before the industrial revolution became possible. Aside from the invention of the steam engine and the availability of iron ore and coal, food preservation first became necessary on a large scale with the industrial revolution. With millions of people in factories separated from food on the farms, there was no other way.

The logistics of getting food to factory laborers in cities led to the development of canning. Open cans were filled with a pre-weighed amount of substance. The filled cans were sterilized by pressurized steam. The heat also expanded the contents and drove out air. When the can was sealed and allowed to cool, the cooling contracted the contents and created a partial vacuum inside the can. Milk was made safe by pasteurizing, heating it past 160 degrees fahrenheit for fifteen seconds before rapidly cooling it to below fifty degrees fahrenheit.

The incredible advances in technology in the twentieth century can be said to have two great underpinnings, new materials and, electronics. It cannot be ignored that meeting the needs of warfare has been a prime mover in the century's technical progress.

MATERIALS

One side of the story of materials in the twentieth century is synthetization, making synthetic substitutes for natural materials, including metal alloys designed for specific purposes. We can do a lot of manipulating with natural rubber, speeding up the vulcanization process with a variety of catalysts called accelerators. Natural rubber can be tailored to the desired properties, such as extra toughness or elasticity, for a specific purpose by choosing an appropriate accelerator for use during the vulcanization process, which is heating the raw rubber with about three percent sulfur. But today, a full three quarters of all rubber used is synthetic. In the case of rubber, the synthetization process became necessary because of the cutting off of natural rubber from south-east Asia during the second world war.

The other side of the materials story is new materials which are entirely synthetic, having no counterpart in nature. The material of the century is certainly plastic in it's many forms. Ethylene is a small molecule with two atoms of carbon and four of hydrogen. When it is heated and compressed to about two thousand atmospheres, many of it's small molecules join together to form a very large molecule, or polymer, with about two thousand atoms called polyethylene. This is a so-called thermoplastic, meaning it changes shape when heated, which is molded into various sheets and containers that you see and use every day. Another small molecule named propylene when treated in a similar way forms polypropylene, which is often used when toughness is required such as to make bags.

In other techniques in which plastics are formed by polymerization, a number of different molecules are made to join by removing molecules of water which divide them. The technique is known as condensation and produces so-called thermosetting plastics, meaning that it does not change shape when heated. The production of bakelite, an early plastic made from coal tar, established this technique.

Special plastics are used extensively in space travel and high-speed aviation. Who can tell what we will end up seeing plastics used for? Photons of light or other electromagnetic radiation may even be usable for the processing of information in place of the electrons in an electric current. Transparent plastics can conduct light just as wires can conduct electricity and the photons would travel faster than the electrons would. Electromagnetic interference would not be a factor and a plastic-based photon computer could possibly be made smaller and lighter.

ELECTRONICS

The technical progress of the century has revolved around electronics like nothing else, resulting in the industrial revolution giving way to the communications revolution. Something is defined as electric when the current flows through a conductor, and defined as electronic when the current is manipulated in a semi-conductor or a vacuum device.

Crude and simple vacuum tubes resulted as an outgrowth of the light bulb, and made possible radio transmitters and amplifiers. But tubes used a lot of power, took up space, generated considerable heat and had to be replaced frequently. The only electronic tubes still in widespread use are the cathode ray tubes in televisions and computer monitors. More advanced electronics such as computers were not practical until the development of the transistor at Bell laboratories.

All transistors are sandwiches of semiconductor chips, usually made of silicon or germanium with each layer "doped" with impurities to give it either an excess or a deficiency of negatively-charged electrons . Bipolar transistors are sandwiches of negative and positive material, either PNP or NPN. All transistors, like vacuum tubes before them, use currents to control other currents and a bipolar transistor has three parts known as emitter, base and, collector.

Aside from bipolar transistors there are field effect transistors, FETs, of which there are several types, and are controlled by voltage instead of current. The three terminals in a FET are called source, gate and drain. Set up appropriately in combination, transistors accomplish tasks such as amplification, oscillation for transmission of radio waves at a particular frequency or, processing of information, in which large numbers of transistors are required.

To make transistors more interesting, there are two classes of operation that a transistor can do, class A and class B. If we want the output wave to have the same shape as the input wave on an oscilloscope, we use class A operation, in which a bias resistance is chosen to ensure that the transistor is about halfway on when there is no input signal. If the controlling input voltage is low, the load resistor in the circuit pulls the output voltage up, such as we would want in a sound amplifier, but the wave is inverted. This is called class B operation.

A transistor's response may not be linear, meaning that an input wave with a higher amplitude would be amplified proportionally more than one with a lower input amplitude, leading to distortion if used to amplify sound. This problem must be compensated for by use of a device known as an operational amplifier.

From the 1950's onward, transistors have made possible a dramatic miniaturization in electronic devices. Transistors look like metal cans the size of small insects but, are not seen as much any more for the simple reason that they can now be made too small to be seen. Chips called microprocessors can hold millions of transistors and are the "brains" of computers where the actual processing of information takes place.

Although these microchips are extraordinarily complex, with more than a dozen layers, the process of manufacture resembles ordinary photography in that electromagnetic radiation, usually in the ultraviolet part of the spectrum is shone through a mask, made of chromium-coated quartz, onto a specially coated wafer of silicon. The coating is hardened if radiation reaches it but remains unhardened if no radiation reaches it. The unhardened coating is then washed away followed by acid etching and metal coating and treating the silicon base with any materials required to give it desired electrical properties. Miniaturization of microchips is only limited by the wavelength of the radiation used to manufacture them. It is possible that in the future, X-rays will be used instead of ultraviolet because of their shorter wavelength.

Certain materials have properties that are especially useful in electronic applications. A material in which a periodic arrangement exists in one or two dimensions but not in all three dimensions is called liquid crystal because the material can flow and form droplets and usually consist of a large molecule with a certain geometric shape. An electronic liquid crystal display is based on the facts that the optical behavior of such a material is dependent on the spatial orientation of it's molecules and that this orientation can be changed at will by application of an electric field. LCDs are used in battery powered devices, including televisions because they require little current.

There has been so many breakthroughs in electronics in the twentieth century that predictions for the future of the field are usually too conservative. Many electronic goods can be made so inexpensively that it is cheaper to just throw them away and get a new one than try to figure out what is wrong with them.

MEDICINE

Medicine is possibly the greatest success story of the twentieth century. Without a longer lifespan, improved health and, freedom from devastating epidemics, the progress that has been made would have been impossible.

Today it is known that all disease is affected by genetics to at least a certain extent. The future should witness gene therapy and drugs to detect and treat a disease genetically before it occurs. Drugs are at

the point now where it takes an average of about twelve years of research and an expenditure of a hundred million dollars or so before reaching the pharmacy shelf, the requirements for the drugs of the future can only get higher.

Surgery is now making use of lasers and proton beams, making possible operations that could not be done in the past. Another example of the application of scientific advances to medicine is Magnetic Resonance Imaging or, MRI for diagnosis of body tissues. Most of the body consists of water, which has two atoms of hydrogen in it's molecule. Carbohydrate and protein molecules also contain many hydrogen atoms. Each different type of body tissue has it's own percent concentration of hydrogen atoms. Every atom, including hydrogen, exerts a small magnetic field, which is random in it's directional orientation and so, the overall magnetic field of billions of atoms is zero due to cancelling. MRI charts body tissues by use of a large electromagnet to line up the body's hydrogen atoms in one direction.

While the atoms are lined up, they spin with a frequency dependent on the power of the electromagnet. A source of electromagnetic waves is set to the frequency at which the hydrogen atoms are spinning in the target tissue. Through resonance, this upsets the alignment of the hydrogen atoms and cause them to radiate waves of the same frequency back.

If the strength of the magnetic field is intentionally varied, atoms along this variation are therefore realigned to fields of varying strength, while giving off varying frequencies of electromagnetic waves. A flat or fully three dimensional image can therefore be produced of each of the body's different tissues.

FLIGHT

The story of the advance of flight from the Wright brothers onward, is an ideal mirror of the advances of the twentieth century as a whole. It also illustrates the role of materials in progress because flight, as much as anything, is dependent on availability of the right materials. The technology of a basic aircraft is not really complex, the most important issue is that the body must be light and very strong at the same time. Without techniques of refining aluminum such as the Hall process, which uses electricity to separate the aluminum from it's ore, flight would not have progressed as it did.

The right power source is also vital, the engine must be light and the fuel compact and high-yield, an aircraft could not fly on a steam engine burning coal. Jet engines have a higher efficiency than any other kind of combustion engine. Turbojet engines have rows of blades, spinning rows alternating with fixed rows, to pull air in, compress it and, move it smoothly to where the fuel is sprayed in and burned.

A jet aircraft today is a palace of high technology. In the most modern aircraft, digital technology is used in the form of a data-bus, a single fiber optic cable connecting every computer and component in the plane. Each device receives and answers data in it's own code. A kind of miniature internet joining the devices of each aircraft.

A branch of the story of aviation in the twentieth century is the helicopter. It is a very versatile craft and the fundamental technology is a variation of than that of an airplane. The angle of each blade is adjusted separately in order to control the craft. The helicopter goes into a simple vertical climb if the angle of all the blades are set the same. To go forward, the angle of each blade is increased when it is at the back and decreased when it comes around the front. This means that there will be more lifting effect at the back than the front and so, the craft will tilt and fly forward.

However, as the craft moves forward, air will be moving faster over the blades moving forward than the blades moving backward and the resulting difference in lifting effect will turn the helicopter to one side. This is corrected by flapping hinges that permit each blade to flap upward, reducing it's lifting power, when it is advancing but not when it is retreating relative to the direction in which the aircraft is flying. A helicopter is limited to a certain maximum speed because the retreating blades are going in the opposite direction to that which the craft is flying and above this maximum speed, less lift effect than is needed to fly will be produced on the side with the retreating blades.

SATELLITES

Since the Soviet Sputnik in 1957, thousands of satellites have been launched. Satellites are also dependent on the right materials, carbon fiber material is used widely in today's satellites. A typical satellite in orbit around the earth moves at about ten times the speed of a jet aircraft. A satellite must be in an orbit at least two hundred miles or so above the earth's surface to avoid destructive friction with the atmosphere. A satellite may be placed in a low orbit before being boosted to a higher orbit by a burst of speed.

If a satellite is not facing the right direction when it is carrying directional antennas or solar cells, it can be re-oriented by either a reaction wheel making use of angular momentum. An electromagnetic coil is used to measure the angular motion of the satellite by interacting with the earth's magnetic field. Satellites tend to have a limited lifespan and the majority of those orbiting the earth now are no longer in use. Five hundred million dollars may be spent on a typical satellite.

Some satellites are used to monitor the earth below. Monitoring may be done from a satellite by simple observation or by sending out radio signals. Monitoring satellites are often placed in polar orbit, in other words, the satellite orbits over the poles rather than the equator. This means that the satellite will pass over every point on the earth's surface on a regular basis so that photographs can be taken or, other types of remote sensing can be done. If desired, the orbit can be calculated so that the sun is always shining when the satellite passes over.

Satellites are extremely useful for navigation. In the SARSAT system, a ship in distress only has to activate a radio transmitter beacon and one of five satellites in orbit sends signals to ground station where the small shift in frequency caused by the relative motion of the ship and the satellite is used to find the exact location of the ship. The latest navigational breakthrough is the global positioning system, G.P.S., set up by the United States military and usable by anyone with a special hand-held device transceiver to pinpoint their position anywhere on earth. G.P.S. satellites work by transmitting their location every thousandth of a second and measuring the time the signal takes to return.

The satellite Echo served as a reflector for signals and Courier received and retransmitted radio signals in 1960. Telstar opened the age of the television satellite in 1962, it orbited the earth rapidly, every 158 minutes. So, a program broadcast over a long distance could only be seen for a brief period before the satellite moved out of range. A communications satellite is typically placed in an equatorial instead of a polar orbit and higher than a monitoring satellite. The early Telstar ultimately ceased operating due to radiation from high-altitude nuclear tests.

The lower a satellite's orbit, the faster it travels, since the earth is rotating at the same time that means that there must be a point at which the satellite will revolve at the same speed as the earth is rotating and if we want a satellite to remain directly overhead, we can place it at this particular altitude. The altitude is 22,300 miles and a satellite at this altitude is in what is known as a geostationary orbit. Meaning that it stays in the same place in the sky relative to the ground below.

Satellites have made possible a great breakthrough in astronomy. No matter how powerful the telescopes that astronomers use from the earth's surface, electromagnetic radiation coming in from space is distorted by the earth's atmosphere, particularly the shorter wavelengths such as visible light. The answer is to get above the atmosphere.

Until there can be astronomical observatories on the moon, satellites in earth orbit will reveal more of the universe.

The infrared astronomical satellite, IRAS collected a vast amount of data in the infrared part of the spectrum that would have otherwise been absorbed by the water vapor in earth's atmosphere. The Hubble space telescope is a breakthrough in astronomy all by itself, multiplying the size of the observable universe. The telescope has five different scientific instruments analyzing the light received from the telescope.

USE OF THE SPECTRUM FOR COMMUNICATIONS

The real essence of the communications revolution has been making use of the electromagnetic spectrum to carry information over distances. A wide range of frequencies can be used for communications from long waves, such as AM radio broadcasts, to microwaves.

The shorter waves can carry a vast amount of information, many video channels or thousands of audio channels. But waves shorter than a certain length cannot be reflected off the earth's ionosphere like longer waves can, meaning that the high-frequency waves which could carry a lot of information are limited to line of sight reception. This limitation has been overcome by use of satellites which receive and then retransmit a signal between two points on the earth's surface which would otherwise be separated by the line of sight limitation.

The popularity of cellular telephones have made radio bandspace ever more scarce and valuable. Cellular phone towers are visible everywhere and each base station is at the center of a hexagonal cell which intersects with other cells. Transmitters are of relatively low power and use the short length microwave area of the spectrum since the signals do not have to travel long distances. When someone riding in a car talks on their cellular phone, the local base station measures the strength of the signal until it drops to a certain level, meaning that the caller is at the cell boundary. A signal is then sent from the original base station through an exchange to the eight bordering cells to monitor the strength of that particular caller's signal and, the base station in the bordering cell which receives the strongest signal is obviously that of the cell into which the caller has driven and takes over the call until the car crosses another cell boundary.

For telephone communication using a cable, fiber optics is replacing standard copper cable because of the incredible amount of information that fiber optic cables can carry. Information is modulated onto visible light, which has a very short wavelength, much shorter than microwaves, sent through glass cables and demodulated at the other end. Combined with a technique known as pulse code modulation, in which a brief sample of a conversation is taken several thousand times a second instead of the conversation being transmitted continuously, and alternated with brief samples of thousands of other conversations sent on the same wire, literally millions of phone conversations, as well as other types of data can be sent over the same cable.

This does not come cheap, the signal in fiber optic cables must be re-amplified at short intervals or the encoded information will be lost. And the special glass used must be extremely pure, it is said that if there could be a wall seventy miles thick of the glass used in fiber optics, you would be able to see a candle on the other side. But we are in a revolution, the communications revolution, and what has to be done gets done.

USES OF THE SPECTRUM OTHER THAN COMMUNICATIONS

The shorter wavelengths carry a lot of energy and can therefore have uses other than communications. X-rays have been around for quite some time and are produced when a beam of electrons is directed into a metal target. Other short wavelengths, such as gamma rays, are used for sterilization.

Microwaves can be used for cooking as well as communications. A microwave oven works a lot like a small nuclear accelerator except that most accelerators accelerate protons while the microwave oven uses electrons. The ovens use a magnetron, a kind of electronic resonator that produces an electromagnetic wave of one fixed frequency, which is supplied with high voltage by a transformer and which has a filament to emit pulses of electrons. The electrons are guided magnetically around a circular path near a number of metal plates at very high speeds. The group of electrons, with a negative charge, induces an opposite positive charge in each metal plates as it passes, which in turn induces a negative charge on it's neighboring plates. The high speed of the electrons is controlled to cause the charge on the metal plates to oscillate between positive and negative to produce waves with a frequency of about 2450 Megahertz.

Metal tubes guide the waves to a rotating dish which spreads the radiation evenly over the food. Microwaves cook food because the molecules of water in the food are polar, they have one side that is more positive and one that is more negative, and so must turn over every time the charge on the metal plates changes. This incessant movement of the food's water molecules generates the heat which cooks the food from the inside out.

Lasers were invented in Britain in 1960 and make use of the spectrum in another way. The word laser is an acronym for "light amplification by stimulated emission of radiation". Lasers were preceded by masers, microwave amplification by stimulated emission of radiation.

A laser consists of a high-intensity flash lamp coiled around a ruby rod, which has a totally reflecting mirror on one end and a partially reflecting mirror on the other end. The distance between the two mirrors must be very precisely set in order to produce constructive interference with regard to the wavelength.

The ruby, the so-called active medium, acts as an optical resonator, in which the lamp starts an avalanche effect of photons, or packets of light, beamed out from the partially reflecting end of the ruby rod. Laser light can be very sharply tuned to a monochromatic frequency and unlike a beam of multichromatic light, spreads barely at all over long distances.

Lasers, with the ability to transmit a vast amount of energy or information over a distance have a wide variety of uses. Combined with fiber optic cable, lasers can be used in laser gyroscopes, in which a pulse of laser light is sent into each end of a coiled, kilometer-long fiber optic cable. Direction is determined by noting where the two pulses meet. Lasers have made a revolution in surgery possible by their use in such things as delicate eye operations. Combined with computers, lasers are used in bar code technology.

The one field of knowledge that has really benefitted from exploitation of the electromagnetic spectrum is astronomy. At the beginning of the twentieth century, astronomical telescopes were limited to the relatively narrow visible part of the spectrum. Radio telescopes were developed later and provided a window on the radio part of the spectrum, useful because longer waves in the radio range are the ones least distorted by the atmosphere. Satellites have made possible full use of the infrared and ultraviolet parts of the spectrum, which if received on the earth's surface would be distorted by the atmosphere.

At the other end of the size scale, microscopes are limited in what they are able to resolve by the wavelength of visible light. No matter how well a visible microscope is made, it cannot resolve objects smaller than the wavelength of light itself, meaning that it is of no use for an optical microscope to have the ability to magnify more than about 1400 times. The breakthrough came by using a beam of electrons, controlled and focused by electromagnetic fields, in place of visible light.

One design of electron microscope is the transmission electron microscope. An intermediate image is formed by a magnetically focused electron beam illuminating the object to be observed then being focused magnetically. Another magnetic focusing apparatus then picks out a desired part of the intermediate image to form a final image on a fluorescent screen or photographically.

Another design of electron microscope is the scanning electron microscope. A focused beam of electrons scans the object to be observed, which knocks secondary electrons from the object, which are collected at a positive electrode. An image can be produced because more secondary electrons are generated when the primary beam strikes a curved edge or a sloping surface than when it hits a flat surface. The amount of secondary electrons generated is automatically calculated for each spot and combined into an image.

NUCLEAR

Anything nuclear from bombs to reactors has gained a bad reputation, even though it is one of the great stories of the twentieth century. However, there is much more to nuclear science. For one thing, the high-energy gamma rays given off by the isotope cobalt-60 is used to sterilize items such as disposible medical supplies.

For another, a common smoke detector is a simpler use of nuclear science. It contains a small piece of radioactive material which gives off alpha particles, one of the three forms of radioactivity. These particles knock electrons out of atoms in the air, forming positive ions, which conduct an electric current between metal plates in the detector. The current is usually supplied by a battery. The detector works by closely monitoring this current, if particles of smoke mix with the ions and interfere with the current, an alarm is triggered.

Whenever there is some kind of flow that must be monitored such as in medicine or industry, radionuclides are useful because it is easy to measure the radioactivity given off and therefore their location. In manufacture of anything in sheet form, whether metal, paper or, plastic, variations in the thickness of the product may indicate a flaw of some kind, and can be continuously measured by placing a radioactive source on one side and a detector on the other side.

Radionuclides are used in research, industry and, medicine and are simply nuclides that are radioactive and therefore decay by giving off one of the three forms of radioactivity. Most are manufactured from one of a wide variety of elements on the periodic table, tailored to special needs. They can be made by bombarding an element with neutrons inside a nuclear reactor to change it to an unstable, radioactive version of the next highest element on the periodic table. This can also be accomplished by hitting the target element with high-energy particles in an accelerator such as a cyclotron.

WARFARE

Since a cure for warfare has yet to be found, the best that can be done is to be prepared for it. The needs of warfare was a powerful driving force behind the technical progress made in the twentieth century and, military preparedness is benefitting from advances in almost all branches of technology.

One of the most publicized cutting edges of military technology is stealth, specially designing military aircraft to make them invisible to radar. Part of the solution is the shape of the aircraft. Flat surfaces and sharp angles, such as wing and tail leading edges and air intakes, are good radar reflectors and designers are seeking smooth, blended shapes for the aircraft body instead.

The other part of the solution to radar avoidance is coating the aircraft body with radar absorbent material. Such material used to be heavy and so, it's use was limited to those specific areas with high radar reflection. Research into new materials has brought about a low-density foam over a mixture of carbon and plastic that can drastically reduce a plane's visibility on radar.

On the other hand, infrared sensors are being considered as an alternative to radar. These sensors detect not only the heat from the airplane's exhaust but the heat buildup on the surface from friction with the air. There is as of yet, no defense against infrared sensors except decoy flares, which cannot fool sophisticated systems.

Other unconventional weapons include carbon fiber strands falling from air-detonated cruise missiles which floated down on Baghdad's electrical centers at the start of the gulf war and plunged the city into darkness.

The real breakthrough in warfare in the information revolution is, as you might expect, information warfare. Ingenious computer programs may be written to do such things as turning off a country's electrical system. Computer viruses and worms are promising weapons which can at least freeze a country's most secure communications networks, forcing it's military to use less secure networks.

LABORATORY ANALYSIS

Two powerful new tools for conventional laboratories in the twentieth century were chromatography and mass spectrometry.

Chromatography analyzes the components of a solution using the fact that a particular absorbent will absorb each component at a different rate because of their differences in solubility. Using a so-called liquid phase with the solid absorbent made possible sharp separation of mixtures because some components of the solution would attach more strongly to the liquid and some to the solid. If a mobile liquid phase is used in the analysis, different components of the solution will move down a column, where they are to be collected, at different rates because they were absorbed by the liquid at different rates.

A mass spectrometer divides a vaporized mixture of atoms according to the masses of the atoms. The sample is made into positive ions by having an electron knocked out of each atom, which are then passed through the poles of a magnet in a vacuum chamber. The sample is separated into it's component atoms because the atoms of each element have a different weight and lighter atoms, or lighter isotopes of the same atom, are deflected more than heavier ones, landing on a screen or photographic plate. The element and ratio of component atoms in the sample can be measured.

PROBLEMS TO BE SOLVED

As far as science and technology have come, there is still plenty to be done. First of all, there is the perpetual problem of finding usable energy that will not destroy the environment. Oil is the largest source of energy, providing about forty percent of the world's total. Natural gas makes up about half that of oil, hydropower around seven percent and nuclear power about five percent. There are over four hundred nuclear plants around the world but their safety is a topic of concern as is their wastes. The sun and wind are renewable and would seem to be obvious answers but, much more research and a fortune in investment is needed before this is possible.

As ever-increasing miniaturization becomes possible, the field of nanotechnology opens before us. This makes all kinds of things possible by manipulating things on a very small scale, such as handling and assembling individual atoms. IBM may have started a new trend in advertising when it managed to spell out it's name in single-file xenon atoms.

Every year, hurricanes wreak havoc in the Carribean and much of the United States. We can warn of approaching storms and can predict the weather a week or so in advance. But stopping such things as Atlantic hurricanes before they start is still in the future. Storms form in Africa when hot, dry air over the Sahara desert collides with moist cool air over sub-saharan Africa, producing a swirling pattern of moving low pressure air. During late summer and fall, the water in the nearby Atlantic ocean is warm and rising and when the low pressure center arrives overhead, the rising air climbs faster still while dropping it's considerable moisture. At the ocean surface, more warm air flows in to take the place of that which has risen and rises as well, while also dropping it's moisture. A self-sustaining system has formed by this point and moves across the ocean as a tropical storm.

Advances in technology do not always originate with research. Many of the improvements in automobiles for example, come from lessons learned in motor sports.

Which, along with the advertising value, is why manufacturers participate, using the racetrack as a laboratory. The concept of disc brakes started in the airline industry, was adapted to auto racing and, finally found it's way into the family car. Fuel injection, aerodynamic bodies, composite construction materials and, much of a car's electronics systems were all ideas pioneered in motor sports.

SCIENTIFIC FRONTIERS

Our pure scientific knowledge has multiplied many, many times in the twentieth century. One of the frontiers is the search for a unified field theory that accounts for all the basic forces; electromagnetism, gravity, the nuclear force and, the weak nuclear force which causes radioactivity. Albert Einstein spent the last thirty years of his life in search of such a theory. It is now believed that every fundamental force has a particle associated with it. Photons are related to the electromagnetic force, for example.

Scientists are still figuring out exactly what happened at the big bang which started the universe. We know that the explosion itself lasted only a few minutes. It is generally believed that matter as we know it emerged after about 300,000 years and that galaxies began forming after a billion years. We can detect the background radiation in the microwave part of the spectrum coming from all directions in the sky from the original explosion. In 1989, a satellite, the cosmic background explorer COBE, was launched especially to study this radiation from the beginning of the universe.

ASTRONOMY

The final frontier is of course, the universe. The great lesson of the twentieth century is just how insignificant our earth really is considering the universe as a whole. Not long after the first communications satellites, human beings first went into earth orbit and then landed on the moon several times. Astronomy is the one science in which laboratory experiments are not directly possible but, numerous robot space probes have explored the solar system and sent back data and photographs. We have already discussed the satellites such as COBE, IRAS and, the Hubble Space Telescope, which serve as revolutionary new observatories above the atmosphere's distortion and interference.

There are planets orbiting other stars beyond our solar system which are too faint to be directly seen from earth. The conventional way of detecting such planets is to measure their gravitational effect on their parent stars, a difficult process. Making use of the rest of the electromagnetic spectrum gives us a new possibility. Although a planet does not give off visible light of it's own that can be seen from earth, it does radiate in the infrared part of the spectrum and points of infrared radiation around stars almost certainly indicates the presence of unseen planets.

A very unconventional type of telescope is the underground neutrino telescope, usually constructed in a disused mine to filter out cosmic rays and other interference. Usually, the massless neutrinos pass right through the earth without stopping. One hundred thousand or so gallons of perchloroethylene in a deep mine will detect neutrinos emitted from the core of the sun because they convert atoms of chlorine into radioactive argon, which can then be counted.

If one thing is certain about the universe, it is that we are only just beginning to learn about what it has to offer.

CHAPTER FOUR

▼

THE COMPUTER

The central icon of the information revolution is the computer, it can best be described as an information manager. The big main-frame computers launched it but it is the personal computer, or PC, upon which the revolution really depends. We could say that the PC got it's start in 1975 when Paul Allen and Bill Gates successfully programmed the primitive Altair computer with the BASIC language. Before that, in 1971, the Intel 4004 became the first microprocessor chip for widespread use. Without such microchips, PC's as we know them would not be possible.

Corporate brands are far more important in computers than in other electronic products. The two big choices in personal computers at this point is IBM clones or MacIntosh. IBM is by far the most popular, especially in business, but Macs still have their core of devotees claiming that they are easier to learn and use and continue to be widely used in advertising and design. The term "PC" (personal computer) is generally understood to refer to IBM machines.

There is also so-called clones of the two main branches of personal computers. Cloning apparently started when a company called Compaq came up with a computer that used the same microprocessor and software as IBM PCs. A now-famous company named Microsoft was started by Bill Gates and grew by writing software for IBM and it's clones. All personal computers consist of the same basic parts.

HARD DRIVES

The hard drive is where information is stored in the personal computer. It consists of metal, usually aluminum, disks or platters with a chemical coating that contains tiny particles of an oxide of a metal having the ability to hold a magnetic charge. Information can be stored because each of the billions of magnetic particles can be oriented in one of two ways, with it's north pole facing the direction the disk spins and the south pole facing the reverse direction or vice versa. This information is written and read by electromagnets in the read and write heads which are located just above and below each disk in the hard drive. Information can also be stored on magnetic tapes but, the data would not be easily accessible at random as it is in a hard drive. Today, magnetic tape is used primarily for backups.

The hard drive in a PC is an example of very high-precision engineering. It must operate in a clean, sealed chamber. The read and write heads have to be so close to the disks as they spin that any dust getting between the two would cause the hard drive to crash. In recent years, rapid progress has been made in making hard drives faster to access information, physically smaller and, with much more memory. It is debatable whether more progress has been made in the performance of hard drives or microchips.

Hard drives use a variety of different methods to communicate with the computer as an interface on the bus, which is the computer's internal communications route. The most common is the integrated drive electronics, or IDE, an improved version of which is the enhanced IDE or, EIDE. A newer method with better performance is SCSI, small computer system interface, useful because it can be used to control a large number of peripheral items on the computer at once, as well as additional hard drives. Still newer methods replacing SCSI is USB, universal serial bus and, firewire.

If a PC has one hard drive, it is called the C: drive. If it has two hard drives, the other is known as the D: drive. In order to be able to store information, the hard drive must first be formatted, divided into sections so that "addresses" on a file allocation table in the disk can be assigned to each batch of information. A hard drive is formatted when it is manufactured. Obviously, the more empty space there is on a hard drive, the less time it will take the computer to call up information.

FLOPPY DISKS

Floppy disks are the disks, enclosed in a plastic case, that are inserted into the computer. The name comes from the fact that the disk inside the plastic case really is floppy. They are usually three and a half inches wide although some of the older five and a quarter inch ones are still around. Information is stored on them the same as on a hard drive, but floppy disks hold much less information than hard drives. Information on floppy disks is naturally less secure than on hard drives because they can get lost as well as be exposed to dirt.

The usefulness of floppy disks is their portability. They are used to transfer data from one system to another, to make backup copies of files or, to install new software on a personal computer. Just as personal computers made it possible for everyone to own a computer, floppy disks make it easy for anyone who still does not have their own computer to use one somewhere else, bringing their data and then taking it with them when they are finished.

Floppy disks are usually pre-formatted when sold for either IBM and clone PCs or for Macs. Although unlike a hard drive, floppy disks can be formatted or reformatted by any brand of personal computer. Storing a floppy near a magnetic field also "formats" it and may erase valuable information.

MEMORY AND IT'S TYPES

This "memory" on hard drives and floppy disks is simply the ability to store information. Aside from the input from the computer user, installed software programs require a certain amount of memory for themselves. Any kind of color graphics requires a great amount of storage space, much more so than words or black and white graphics.

Data stored in the computer's binary language is measured in "bytes". A byte consists of eight "bits". A bit is one binary piece of information. Binary means "two choices", which comes from the fact that information is stored on the computer's hard drive or floppy disk in the form of millions of magnetic particles which can each be pointed in one of two directions by the read and write heads. The two possible states of each tiny magnetic particle, either north or south pole facing forward, and therefore each bit of information is referred to as a 1 or a 0. This is called a base two number system in contrast to the base ten system we commonly use. In a byte, a set of eight bits, there are 256 possible combinations of 1s and 0s because two multiplied by itself eight times is 256.

There are two basic types of memory used in a PC; ROM and RAM, read only memory and, random access memory. The type in the hard drive is read only memory, when you create a file and then save it, the file is placed in the ROM of the hard drive by the read and write heads in a certain format address. ROM is also available in chips, with data permanently encoded by the manufacturer or, programmable by a process called programmable ROM or, PROM. The capacity of a computer's hard drive can often be increased by installing a memory card.

Random access memory, RAM, is in microchips, which means that unlike the hard drive, it has no moving parts. RAM is the computer's front-line memory. RAM chips in new computers come in groups of nine sold on a PC card called a SIMM, single in-line memory module. There are two kinds of RAM, depending on the construction of the microchips, dynamic RAM, D-RAM and static RAM, S-RAM.

D-RAM chips use thousands of tiny capacitors built into silicon chips, all connected to tiny transistors which control the flow of current into and out of them. Reading D-RAM means that the current must flow out of the capacitors and so be erased, the information in the chip must be maintained by a process known as refreshing. S-RAM chips use tiny flip-flop circuits, meaning that they have two possible states, to store bits of data. S-RAM is not erased every time it is read like D-RAM is so, it is faster although it is more expensive. S-RAM is used often for so-called cache memory programs and in situations where speed is very important.

RAM does not have much storage capacity compared to the computer's hard drive and is intended only for short-term memory. Everything in RAM chips is erased when the computer is turned off. Software programs need a certain amount of RAM to function and the more RAM a computer has, the more applications can be run at the same time.

Hard drive space and RAM can be interchangeable. A portion of the hard drive can be made to act as RAM and is known as virtual memory or a swapfile. ROM, as in hard drive space can also be purchased on chips and installed on the motherboard.

The hard drive of a computer is formatted and information is filed in pre-defined clusters. Data is stored in empty clusters upon input when data is saved and may be scattered across the hard drive in different available clusters. As time goes on and you add and delete files and uninstall programs, your hard drive gets very cluttered. The computer gets much slower to call up given files because the read and write heads must search all over the hard drive to find them. This is known as fragmentation and the answer to this is to run a defragmentation program on your computer every few weeks.

If more room is needed for information in a hard drive or floppy disk, a process known as compression can be utilized. Although the storage capacity can be considerably increased by using a compression program, some other kinds of programs, especially graphics, do not work as well on a compressed disk. Even when compression is used, some people like to leave at least a portion of the hard drive uncompressed.

Computers are always subject to new innovations. To speed up the computer, programs known as "disk cache" have been developed. These programs are based on the fact that information stored in RAM chips is accessible much more quickly than that on the hard drive. Cache programs try to predict what information is likely to be needed next and move it up to RAM chips from the hard drive in advance, so that it will be available much more quickly.

THE MOTHERBOARD AND COMPONENTS

Like a town square, the motherboard functions as the meeting place of the computer's components. The most important component on the motherboard is the central processing unit, the CPU, where the computer's actual processing of data takes place. The CPU in a PC is one of the microchips that we have already examined. Without the mass production of inexpensive microchips, there would be no PC revolution. The term CPU also refers to the cabinet in which the motherboard and the microchip reside.

There are two basic designs for a computer's CPU microchips, CISC and RISC. Complex instruction set computing, CISC, tends to handle data in larger chunks than RISC, reduced instruction set computing. The RISC mode appears to be less complex, faster and, uses physically smaller chips. The issue holding back chips manufactured for the RISC mode seems to be compatibility with existing software and hardware.

A computer's monitor is essentially the same thing as a television screen. Both consist of a cathode ray tube, a CRT, in which a beam of electrons is fired from the back of the tube toward the inside of the screen. The tube, like all vacuum tubes, has all the air removed so that atoms of nitrogen or oxygen will not absorb the electrons in the beam. The electron beam is precisely controlled by a magnetic field and sweeps across the screen many times a second.

The screen has many thousands of pixels, dots which glow in a certain shade or color when the electron beam hits it. The exact shade or color produced by each pixel depends on the intensity of the electron beam and what part of the pixel it lands on. In color TV, each pixel consists of three areas, each being of one of the primary colors, from which any color can be displayed by mixing. As the electron beam is being guided across the screen, it is also being modulated and fine tuned to send just the right information to each pixel in the screen.

The motherboard contains a video controller that modifies the signal from the CPU into commands that can be displayed on the screen on the computer's monitor. This video controller may be built directly into the motherboard or, may be inserted into the computer in the form of an expansion card.

STARTING THE COMPUTER

As soon as the computer is started, it automatically undergoes a POST, a power-on self-test, to check that all components are operational. An alarm can be triggered if everything is not all right but a POST is only intended for the most obvious kinds of malfunctions.

The BIOS of a computer, the basic input-output system, is programmed into a ROM microchip and controls the start-up procedure. It quickly does the essential sorting out of the computer's hardware and software, which could be of thousands of possible combinations and brand names and would render the computer non-functional if not compatible. When the computer starts, the necessary components of the operating system are loaded from the hard drive to RAM.

COMPACT DISKS

CD-ROMs are so-called because they use read-only memory, data can be accessed from them but they cannot be written on. They are five and a quarter inch platters that go into a special drive in the computer. The big advantage of compact disks is their tremendous memory capacity.

Compact disks work using a very small laser beam, operating from a laser diode which can be brought to a very sharp focus, trained on a metallic surface on the disk. The surface has millions of tiny depressions alternating with flat areas, these are called pits and lands and are used to store the information in binary form instead of the magnetic particles in the hard drive of a computer. The pits, the depressions, reflect laser light differently than the lands, sometimes called flats, the flat areas. This difference is detected and modulates an electric current which varies according to whether the beam goes over a land or a pit. The result is processed by the computer in the same way as if data had been read from the magnetic particles on a hard drive. Compact disks are used for music and other multimedia applications simply because of their vast memory capacity.

If a compact disk in the computer was made to spin at constant speed, the outer portion of the disk would move faster than the inner portion and, the lands and pits would have to be much closer together in the inner part of the disk to convey the same amount of data. This is compensated for by varying the speed of the disk according to where the detector is so that the disk is always moving over the detector at the same speed.

A compact disk differs from a hard drive in it's formatting. The radial tracks and sectors on a hard drive make access to data fast but is wasteful of space. Since data on a compact disk is always read sequentially, speed of access is not a factor as it is on hard drives and so, a spiral format is used on compact disks that is much more efficient with space.

Aside from compact disks, digital video disks, DVDs, are being used for multi-media applications. Intended for storing movies, DVDs have a storage capacity far above even compact disks.

EXPANDABILITY AND PERIPHERALS

The needs of every computer user are different. Expandability is the room available in the computer for the addition, if necessary, of peripheral devices or the extra memory and other features available in card form. Anything additional requiring an electronic computer card naturally depends on the number of unoccupied expansion slots. Additional hard drives can be installed on a computer by the use of a hard drive controller card if there is the physical space for them. Aside from additional hard drives, flash storage is also available. A flash storage card is mobile as is a floppy disk but, it has much more storage space and has more physical ruggedness, some flash storage cards require special software to use but others do not.

There are a variety of scanners that can be attached to a computer to input data directly from a hard copy, which means printed on paper, most often for use with graphics. Handheld scanners are moved directly over the document by hand. Flatbed scanners resemble photocopiers in design. Sheetfed scanners are cylindrical and the document is rolled in to be inputted into the computer. There are scanners especially designed for photographs and others for slides.

A computer operating system using a graphical user interface, a GUI, requires a mouse. Mice from different manufacturers have one or two or sometimes three buttons. The left button is used for the most common functions. To use a mouse on a computer requires first of all, a program where use of the mouse is applicable and, software called a device driver telling the computer how to use the mouse along with the port for the mouse to be plugged into the computer. Every piece of computer hardware must have a driver, software instructions to the computer's central processor concerning the operation of the hardware device.

PRINTERS

The most important peripheral on a computer is the printer which produces a hard copy, or printed copy of the information on the computer. Printers are usually classified as impact or non-impact, the impact varieties are usually noisier and with poorer quality output but are less expensive and more rugged and can usually print on continuous-feed paper while non-impact printers print one sheet at a time. Dot matrix is the most common impact printer. Ink jet, which prints by shooting ink through a matrix, and the more expensive laser printers, which fuse powdered ink called toner to the paper, are non-impact. A barrel printer is a large impact printer used in industry. The printer, of whatever type, is the piece of computer hardware most likely to need repair or maintenence.

One complaint about printing is how slow it can be. But that is due to the software and the available memory in the computer rather than the printer itself. A printing job requires a lot of computer disk space and if this space is not available, the task will take time. Anything color, and using a greater variety of colors, will take the printer longer to deal with, just as it takes up much more space in the computer's memory.

COMPUTER LANGUAGES

Some small computers are designed to do only one task, the processes of which are built in to the computer, this is known as hard wiring. In all other cases the computer, which can do a vast number of things, needs to be told what to do. Programs are written to make the computer do different things and are stored in the computer's memory, a process called programming. The physical parts of the computer, the ones that can be touched, are called hardware. The instructions guiding the computer are known as software. A floppy disk is hardware, the application it is used on is software. The vast majority of computer problems are software conflicts.

The computer itself only understands the directional orientation of the magnetic particles used to store information and the 1s and 0s that they represent, called machine code. Each particle of information is known as a bit and eight of those are known as a byte. Every item on the computer's keyboard is represented by a different sequence of eight 1s and 0s, taking up a byte, this is known as the ASCII code. By using thousands and millions of bytes, very complex instructions can be coded into a computer.

Computer languages are prearranged instructions for the computer that can be combined in different patterns to make the computer do many different things. There are computer languages for all kinds of different purposes. A common language is BASIC, which stands for beginners all-purpose symbolic instruction code. BASIC was derived from FORTRAN, formula translation, an early computer language. BASIC is a language for mathematical operations and consists of three parts; commands, variables and, functions. Lines in a BASIC program are numbered ten apart and more things can be added later on because the program is run in numerical order. BASIC is useful because parts of a program can be run to see if they work before the entire program is completed, there are many dialects of BASIC. Other older languages are COBOL and ALGOL, newer languages include C, C+, C++. HTML or hypertext markup language was developed for web pages. TCP / IP, transfer control protocol / internet protocol, is the computer language of the internet and is used to process and send data.

OPERATING SYSTEMS

A computer must have an operating system, a complex software program that oversees everything the computer does. The operating system enables all the hardware components of the computer to work together and translates any tasks the computer is involved in into something the computer can understand. The most popular operating system was Microsoft DOS, disk operating systems. It was the basis for the famous Windows system, which made use of a revolutionary concept called graphical user interface, GUI, the use of a mouse, icons and, dialog boxes instead of the old screens of solid text. A system like windows takes up a lot of space in a computer's memory and did not become practical until such memory was available. Like any other software, it runs better when more memory is available. UNIX is the complex operating system used to run the internet.

Operating systems, like any other software, comes in floppy disks from which data is transferred to the hard drive using a special procedure. Software versions are given numbers such as DOS 6.0, Windows 1.0, Windows 3.0, Windows 3.1 and, Windows 95 or 98. The numbers before the decimal point indicate major upgrades, while that after the decimal point indicates minor upgrades in the software by the manufacturer.

PROGRAMS

A computer program is a set of instructions that makes a computer do something. It is software just as the operating system is but it's purpose is to actually get some useful work done with the computer. The terms program, application and, software are sometimes used interchangeably. Printer languages such as PCL and Postscript are the programs in the computer that control the printer, the printer drivers in contrast are programs providing communication between the printer and the computer.

Documents can be divided into four categories; word processing, graphics, spreadsheets and, databases. A spreadsheet is used for accounting, a database is a store of information like a phone book. There are programs available for each and, many such as Microsoft office which offer one each of all of them. Any variety of insertions and combinations can be produced. A communications program to send e-mail or, a desktop publishing program, which is an advanced word processor program may be included.

A vast variety of computer programs are available. There are programs to utilize the computer's memory more fully. There are programs to compress data to take up less space in the memory. Cache programs for the computer use more easily accessible memory in RAM microchips to speed up the computer. Cache programs for the printer set aside memory in the computer for use in helping to speed up printing.

Anything as popular and as complex as computers will inevitably be found in use for shady purposes. There are programs such as Trojan horses, which are secretly concealed in larger programs and can be activated secretly to steal or plant data. Viruses are programs that can reproduce themselves and spread rapidly through computer networks, rendering information useless. A worm is similar to a virus in that it spreads through systems, it reproduces itself until stored information is meaningless data. Logic bombs are instructions set in advance to commit some destructive act, such as deleting important data, if a certain name is added or deleted from a database, for example.

NETWORKS OF COMPUTERS

It is possible to connect computers into networks to share information. In office buildings there are LANs, local area networks, and WANs, wide area networks. Mainframe computers usually have terminals resembling PCs from which information can be inputted into the system or accessed, but these are not real networks of equal computers. A network must have some system to referee conflicting requests for data and whatever else the network has to offer. There are network adapter cards for the member computers, called nodes, clients or, workstations. A network needs an operating system just as individual computers do. A variety of possible patterns and techniques are used in connection of computers, they can be attached in a ring or attached to a file server in the center. A system of switching and an exchange similar to that used with telephones would be possible. Better yet, the computers can be attached to one cable called a bus from which each computer extracts the data electronically addressed to it.

THE STORY OF THE INTERNET

If we can connect computers in networks to share data, what if we could connect computers all over the world to share data and communications? We can and it is called the internet. The incredible flow of data that has resulted is known as the information superhighway. This is accessible to virtually anyone in the world and is the main vehicle of the information revolution.

In 1969, the U.S. government began work on a network of computers all over the country designed to survive a nuclear attack, named ARPANET for Advanced Research Projects Administration Network. Mainframe computers at big universities were the first nodes in the network, using it for research purposes.

The secret of the network was to be it's numerous nodes and the web of connections between them. The theory was that data could be sent from one node to another in small packets of information that could be sent by any number of routes through the web of connections to it's destination and then reassembled. TCP / IP was developed to divide the data into packets and encode destination addresses. If a nuclear attack occured, much of the web of connections and nodes may be wiped out but, communications could still proceed through whatever was left. Kind of like shooting bullets into a spider web, some of the web will be destroyed but it would be difficult to destroy all of it.

In 1983, MILNET, the military network, split off from ARPANET, leaving the rest of the network to civilians. The National Science Foundation, the NSF, operated the network for a few years but it became known as the internet and open to anyone by the boom in personal computers. The internet was simply too big of a project for capitalism alone to produce. No corporation would have decided that it could make a profit by constructing something as large as the internet.

Standardization was also vital to the operation of any large network, even if the internet could have came into being without the government, it would not have grown as fast as it did without the adoption of a standard operating system for the network, UNIX, and TCP/ IP. The TCP part of the language slices the information into packets and decides which way to route each one across the web of connections. This language was not developed commercially and so is open to anyone and, any corporate brand of computer can access the internet.

THE WORLD-WIDE WEB

The world wide web is a kind of graphical interface on the internet, resembling the way the Windows operating system serves as an easier to use graphical interface on the older DOS operating system. The WWW as it is commonly known, was developed at CERN, the nuclear research center in Switzerland, in the early 1990s. It was originally used by physicists but became accessible to the public when a system of software named Mosaic was developed to make it easy to use.

Internet and web page addresses are to be seen everywhere. The endings of internet addresses indicate what kind of institution it is; .com for commercial, .gov for governmment, .mil for military, .edu for educational, .org for some other type of organization. On web addresses, the http stands for hypertext transfer protocol.

What is great about the WWW is it's use of links, called hypertext, to simplify the search for information about a particular topic. This helps a lot because related information is often categorized under different headings. Suppose you wanted to find all the information available about the industrial revolution. Some information would be found under inventions, more information would be categorized under history, more still under biographies of people involved in the revolution in different ways. Finding all possible information about it in all the different categories, even with the internet, could be very time consuming and difficult.

But, what if links were provided in each available document to other documents in the web with related data? This is just what the WWW does using the standard language called HTML, Hypertext Markup Language, which contains codes telling the web browsers how and where to find related documents. All the user has to do is use the mouse to click on a highlighted and underlined word in any document to go to another document which the word indicated. Netscape Navigator and Microsoft internet explorer have arisen as web browsers. There are search engines to find information on the WWW such as Yahoo, Lycos and, Webcrawler.

Before the development of the WWW, information had to be reached using older and more difficult applications. Telnet is one such application that connects a computer with a remote computer, making your computer into a terminal of the distant one using TCP / IP. Using this application, you were in effect operating a far away computer using the keyboard of your own computer.

FTP, file transfer protocol used remote log-in the same as telnet and it also uses TCP / IP to send or retrieve files from distant computers. FTP is more advanced than e-mail in that nothing needs to be written out for the purpose of being sent if it is already in the computer.

Archie is a system to find files available for remote downloading. The Archie system consists of central computers called servers which build a database of retreivable files available for use. When a file located by Archie is sought, it is found and obtained using FTP.

Gopher is another application with a network of computers. It provides menus and sub-menus of available files and unlike Archie, retrieves the files itself. It was named Gopher because it "goes for" the information. Veronica is another application and it's purpose is to search Gopher computers and provide a menu, since it may be impossible for a person to know which one of the many Gopher computers the sought-after file is on.

WAIS, Wide Area Information Server, is another search vehicle created before the WWW. WAIS searches individual documents and creates a database grouped by subject to assist in searching for information on a particular topic.

The advent of the WWW brought a convenient interface for searching the internet and as you can see in the multitude of older search vehicles, greatly simplified things.

ON THE INTERNET

The internet is accessible from any personal computer. The first thing that is needed is a modem to connect the computer to the telephone network, each computer hooked into the internet should have it's own telephone line. The word "modem" comes from modulate and demodulate, which is what the modem does. Telephone wires carry analog signals while computers work in digital signals and, a modem translates from one into the other whenever electronic data comes in or goes out.

A modem can be external and plug in to the computer or, be inside the computer in the form of a card. A modem has a certain speed at which it transmits information known as it's baud rate. A baud is one bit per second and modem speeds are usually measured in thousands of bits per second or, kilobauds. Common modem speeds for the late 1990s were 14.4, 28.8 and, 33.6 kilobaud. Needless to say, the faster, the better.

The two main ways for a PC user to access the internet are internet service providers or commercial on-line services such as AOL, America On Line, Microsoft network and formerly, Compuserve. An internet service provider will usually just connect you to the internet with a choice of either shell versus slip or PPP access. The simpler shell access turns your computer into a terminal of the internet provider service's server computer. Slip or PPP access from an internet service provider makes your computer into a full-fledged member of the internet.

The on-line services offer news, information, e-mail, chat rooms and, special interest topics among many other things. E-mail is easily the most popular use of the internet, there are several applications to send it such as Eudora, Netscape and Pine, on-line services contain one or another for it's users.

There are thousands of software programs for a computer that can be downloaded from the internet. freeware is that which is given away free. Shareware is that which you buy after trying it on your computer and are usually simple programs which the big software companies would not find it worth marketing.

BULLETIN BOARD SYSTEMS

A bulletin board system, or BBS, is used to share information between it's users and is usually accessed by dialing a phone number. A BBS may have either one computer and many phone lines or, a computer for each phone line. A bulletin board system may or may not be attached to the internet. There are database BBSs for information, message BBSs, software program BBSs with programs to be downloaded and, chat BBSs for real-time conversations. Usenet is a system of bulletin board systems on the internet with facilities for over twenty thousand topical discussion groups. Netnews refers to electronic newsgroups on the internet. This is where people with common interests can leave messages to each other.

As far as it has come, the computer revolution is still in it's childhood and, the internet in it's infancy.

CHAPTER FIVE

▼

A TALE OF TWO CAMELS

It is this incredible technical progress that has brought about the commoner syndrome. If civilization did not make progress, capitalism could never have gotten started and you would probably be living in a cave right now. But fortunately that was not the case and the discoveries, advances and, breakthroughs mankind has made have opened up entire new fields of knowledge and technology.

A society of rigidly stratified classes could only exist until the explosion of knowledge in the twentieth century. The rapid advance of technology has brought the voracious need for skills to do many new tasks, while at the same time, increasing the skill requirement level of the already established tasks. This would be simply impossible without tapping the brainpower and skill potential of increasing numbers of commoners, in contrast to past eras.

We are now in a time when knowledge and technology rules the day, as opposed to traditional smokestack industries, it is sometimes known as the third wave. Agriculture, as opposed to simple gathering, being the first wave and, the industrial revolution being the second wave. Even in warfare, a nation of athletes battling a nation of technical geniuses would be no contest.

Human society is a pyramid just like the food chain in nature. However, humans are unique in that we can store knowledge, transmit it, and apply it to ever more sophisticated technology in order to advance our capabilities. Nature's pyramid is fixed in it's order but society's is not. The result of technical progress is a lowering of the line on the pyramid separating elite from commoner, meaning more elites at the top and fewer commoners at the bottom as long as the way in which we define commoner and elite remains constant.

The need for elites in today's economy at the expense of commoners can be seen in the supply and demand factor of the labor marketplace. But it goes much deeper than that. It is not only a part of the supply and demand pendulum, It is part of the advancement of human society. We could say that it involves the pyramid of society itself rather than just the relatively temporary pendulum governing the demands of the marketplace.

It resembles every great revolution of human society. It is like living and working on one floor of a building and being told that your floor will be closing and being forced to move one floor up as space on the higher floor opens up for you.

That is what happened following the stone ages as people learned to plant the crops they needed instead of wandering around looking for a good place to gather food. This was called the agricultural revolution and it led to the construction of permanent buildings instead of temporary shelters, which resulted in civilization as we know it. People were forced to "move up" from their old way of life to a more efficient one.

That is what happened during the industrial revolution when people moved up from feudalism. The pyramid structure did not change in that there were still the few at the top and the many at the bottom. But there was a drastic change in the way of life and work for everyone.

Progress in knowledge and technology is always brought about by elites. That is one of the criteria of an elite, proximity to the cutting edge. The thing holding back many third world countries today is certainly not a shortage of labor, it is a shortage of professionals. Generally, commoners look for jobs or start small low-technology enterprises. Elites advance the technology level and enable many enterprises and society as a whole to expand. As population increases, elites are needed to bring about a corresponding increase in the economy on which all the people depend.

You could compare it to water rising in a tree or a large pyramid game. People move up making room for those below to move up and more people to move in to the game. The tree has different branches corresponding to different sectors of the economy. Those people who do not move up in a reasonable period of time hold things up and are ultimately pushed aside.

As in all the real economic revolutions in which the human economic pyramid itself progresses, as opposed to conditions caused by temporary fluctuations in the pendulum of market forces, the entire workforce must move up at some point. Elites too must learn new things and assume new positions. The elite positions of today are certainly not the end of all things. Some day, elites will become commoners, not by nature but by definition. But for the commoners of today, the future is already in sight- the elites of today.

THE DEMAND FOR ELITES

Progress to this point has brought us one group of people that advance technology and the economy and perform other high-level tasks and cannot be easily replaced. We have another group that maintains society and although their tasks are necessary, the individual workers can be easily replaced.

The genius of capitalism is that it uses market forces to show us what is needed, the law of supply and demand. Right now, the market is demanding more elites. If there are ever too many elites, the market will give an indication of that. The first sign of a change in human society will show up in the pendulum of supply and demand. But this change is irreversible and more on a par with the great economic revolutions of the past, rather than the temporary market fluctuations. In other words, it is an issue of fundamental change in the human pyramid itself rather than the supply and demand pendulum, even though that is where it first showed up.

Technology has advanced to where worker skills are now proportionally more important than natural resources compared with the past. Just take a look at the technology in use today, we not only have to know how to use it but also how to design and produce it. Much of it is the direct result of the communications revolution set off by the industrial revolution and the larger, more complex market system it brought. The commoner, his country cousin the peasant, and his predecessor the serf, predominated when short-term survival was an issue for many people. Now that society has advanced to where it is not, there is room and need for more elites.

What shows set in the future have you watched? Lost in space? Star Trek? The Jetsons? Try for a moment to figure out how the world could get to a level something like that. With a lot of elites acquiring knowledge and, many more to utilize it. That is the only possible way.

An ideal definition of an elite is simply the kind of person the world will need more of in the future.

THE RESULTS OF PROGRESS

There is no doubt that the skill factor of many commoner tasks as well as the workers' educations has drastically increased. If a typical commoner was time-transported back a century, he would be able to tell the elites a few things. But society has made progress on two fronts, it has improved the commoners' skills while at the same time, reducing the need for commoners.

The elite / commoner ratio of a society could be considered as a kind of polygamy. One elite for several commoners. The more advanced the country, the higher the ratio or, we could say, the lower the line on the pyramid separating commoner and elite. Many of the wealthier nations import "guest workers" in various ways to fill the lower portion of the pyramid if the line is too low to provide enough of these workers to meet local demand.

Yet, progress also means that if a worker's skill level stays the same while that of the world advances, he in effect falls behind. It is similar to a wave circle expanding from a splash in a pool of water. Like the splash made by the start of the industrial revolution in the pool of time. As the wave front expands, any point that is within the circle and at an "average" location from where the splash took place, must continuously move in the same direction as the wave or "fall behind".

Technology, particularly the computer and automation, has rapidly increased the sum total of the world's skill, and in doing so, traded commoner for elite. The very purpose of automation in industry is to eliminate commoners. It may seem to you that the blacksmiths of the 1800's have been obsolete for quite some time. Actually, the world needs blacksmiths more than ever, except that now the blacksmiths are machines. They still exist, but like some kind of ghosts, blacksmiths exist only in the form of circuits, electric motors and, software.

The purpose of technology is to make life easier and it does. But it works on all levels, it also makes life easier for those running industries. Which means that it affects the positions and lives of laborers. Starting with the industrial revolution, technology fed on itself and multiplied and moved fast enough to uproot the workplace.

At the beginning of the twentieth century it was laissez-faire capitalism running wild, in the view of many, mercilessly exploiting the poor workers. At the end of the twentieth century, it is technology that is running wild. The bad news is that technology cannot be reformed like capitalism. The good news is that this is not the gilded age of capitalism and upward mobility is open to anyone. But a commoner cannot simply declare himself an elite, the required skills and knowledge must be mastered.

The commoners are being electrocuted like condemned men. Not literally of course, but in the myriad of machines running on electric motors and used in the automation of factories. Machines that can work faster, more accurately and in less space than hundreds of laboring commoners ever could. And who do not complain, call in sick, go on strike or, demand a raise, except for the few who must still be kept around to feed and tend the machines. But they know how easily they could be replaced.

BUBBLES ALWAYS BURST

The swings of the capitalist pendulum away from the central peak of maximum efficiency occasionally create what are sometimes called "bubbles". These bubbles usually occur in the stock market and sometimes in the real estate market. What these bubbles basically mean is artificially high prices. But bubbles always burst sooner or later and these are no different. The 1980's were one of the golden ages of bubbles, but the stock market burst in the October 1987 crash and, the real estate market in 1990. The capitalist pendulum will only go in one direction for so long. When the pendulum swings back down and the bubble bursts suddenly, it is called a correction because it returns the market to prices that are more realistic.

Things like the stock market and real estate market are concise and, this makes it so that they can burst and fall suddenly and rapidly. Other aspects of the economy such as the middle class and socialism are much more nebulous and imprecise and while they are just as subject to the market forces as the stock and real estate market, they will not rise as fast, burst suddenly or, drop as fast as the concise and precise stock and real estate markets.

Socialism is declining across the world as we have seen because it has done it's job and according to capitalist market forces, is no longer worth the price. The middle class in America is also definitely shrinking. We saw how the distribution of families in our economy can be best displayed by the often-used statistical shape known as the bell curve. The term "middle class" refers not to the line of work a person is in, as the terms "commoner" and "elite" does, but in their earnings from whatever work they do. The middle class shrinking means that there is more rich people at the top, more poor people at the bottom, at the expense of fewer people in between.

THE HUMPS OF TWO CAMELS

Have you ever been intrigued by the camels at a zoo? There are two major types of camel, the dromedary and the bactrian camel. The most obvious difference between them is that the dromedary has one hump and the bactrian camel has two, with a space in the middle. That is an ideal model for the economy, it is moving from the shape of the hump of a dromedary to the shape of the humps and the space between of the bactrian camel. The phenomenon of the middle class is not going to suddenly burst like the stock or real estate market. But that is only because it is much larger and more complex as well as more nebulous. Yet, there is little doubt that the middle class will end up very much reduced.

The fantastic advances in society brought about by the explosion of knowledge and technology in the twentieth century would have been utterly impossible in the stratified society of 1900. Far more brainpower and entrepreneurial energy than that possessed by the few elites at the top would be needed. The commoners were born with minds and had ambitions just as elites had, and this had to be at least partially utilized. If it had not been, it is almost certain that men would never have landed on the moon, you would not be able to send e-mail over the internet or fly across the world easily, and I would probably not be writing this on a word processor.

However, during the twentieth century, descendents of the commoner families of 1900 did not all move up from their positions of that time to the same extent. While there is a much higher elite / commoner ratio in today's society than there was then, the ratio of commoners has not gone down anything like as fast as the need for commoners. When a commoner works while the world advances, the relative skill of that commoner's task continuously diminishes and he falls behind. A falling that sooner or later translates into falling from the middle class.

There are four possible categories for a job to fall into pertinent to wages and skill. High-wage, high-skill jobs; high-wage, low-skill jobs; low-wage, high-skill jobs and; low-wage, low-skill jobs. The only two that make any sense are the first and the last ones. The law of supply and demand makes that perfectly clear. The pendulum of capitalism is not always at the peak of efficiency and it's up and down swings can bring them into being temporarily, as a stage, but they cannot exist permanently.

The one great factor producing the large middle class in America in the latter half of the twentieth century was the conditions in the outside world. The world was either trying to slowly recover from devastation in war, undergoing the transition from imperial times, either losing colonies or adapting to independence or, simply just not being in the same league as the United States. At one point in the 1950's a full half of the world's industrial output incredibly came from a single country, the United States. The high-wage, low-skill jobs that usually do not exist for long stayed around long enough to build a large middle class in America. Those families that used this as an opportunity to gain a higher, more secure position will be in the upper "hump" as the middle class shrinks, those families that did not will inevitably fall into the lower hump at some point.

The middle class was much more than a fluke brought about by the fluctuations of capitalism. It served a vital role. I like to put the middle class in the same category as socialism, discussed earlier. That of a transition stage rather than a permanent condition, comparable to adolescence. The middle class is certainly, to some extent, the product of socialism. Labor unions can be considered as a kind of facet of socialism from the grass roots rather than from the top down. The middle class served to give people whose parents or grandparents had lived a lean life as commoners a chance to become the elites that the growing economy really needed, or at least have their children do so.

Once a capitalist economy gets rolling, it seems to have a mind of it's own as the law of supply and demand contiuously works to find the peak of maximum efficiency. It is a mind that proved far superior to those running the bureaucracies in communist countries. As we saw, the society of today would be impossible without harnessing the brainpower and entrepreneurial ambitions of millions of people whose parents or grandparents had been commoners. The certain amount of surplus money that people in the middle class can come up with went to pay college tuitions and start businesses. Had this not happened, the progress achieved in the second half of the twentieth century would simply not have happened.

That is of course, not the only vital role the middle class has played. It made possible the progress and expansion of the economy in another way. Without the middle class as consumers, as well as producers, the economy would not have expanded and progressed as it did. Those millions of high-wage, low-skill jobs and the income they brought to the millions of families, made possible by conditions in the outside world compared with in the United States, created the insatible demand for continuously improved goods that kept the economy growing and drove technology to ever-higher levels. Many American products also went to fill demand in other countries and the United States remained a net exporter for a long time, which gave a big boost to it's industries making possible these high-wage, low-skill jobs.

Without this middle class-driven expansion outward and upward, it is doubtful if communism would have ruptured while struggling to keep up. Somewhere along the line, industrialists must have realized that as long as all the other industries gave into union demands to raise wages, workers with more money to spend will buy more products, enabling the industries and the entire economy to expand.

But now, all of the reasons for the existence of the middle class are gone as surely as they are for socialism. The outside world as a whole has narrowed the gap with America and much of it, particularly western Europe, has caught up. Since 1985, America has been a net importer rather than exporter. The middle class has served as a springboard for many people whose parents or grandparents were commoners to move up to being elites, the others who have not made such progress are in the process of falling back out of the middle class, forming the two humps when it is displayed graphically instead of the bell curve.

Capitalism gets it's name because it is "capital" that is used to start or expand a business. It requires an investment of money to make it possible to make money in the long run. In large corporations, this capital is usually raised by selling shares of itself in the form of stock. This means that the entire existence of the middle class in the postwar years can be looked at as a very large-scale outlay of capital with the aim of a massive expansion of the economy. The millions of high-wage, low-skill jobs that made possible commoners or, their children rising up to swell the middle class were artificial according to the basic principles of capitalism. But in 1950, communism was an ever-expanding domain showing no signs of reversing anytime soon. You can be sure that it was the middle class, as artificial as it was, that won the cold war.

However, now we have many more people in the upper class or closer to it and, the spending of the traditional middle class is no longer needed and the spending of the traditional middle class is not needed as much to stimulate large-scale expansion of the economy. Along with these other reasons is the basic fact that the world gets more high-tech every year and the many low-skill commoner jobs, at least those paying high wages are no longer viable. The capitalist market forces have spoken very clearly.

As we have seen, the term "middle class" is a term of earnings rather than occupation. When we say "the middle class is shrinking", this does not mean there will not be a middle class, but it does mean that whatever middle class is left will not be accessible to those with low-skill jobs. In a graphical representation, the familiar bell curve resembling the hump of a dromedary is giving way to the double humps separated by a gap of the bactrian camel.

The remarkable thing is that the whole idea of a middle class is incongruent with the basic pyramid that has always defined human society with it's few elites at the top and the many commoners below. As we have seen, the technical progress that accompanied the postwar expansion of the economy, which would have been impossible without tapping the brainpower and entrepreneurial ambitions of millions of people of commoner background, has created a multitude of new job categories that has somewhat blurred the traditional division between commoner and elite. But certainly not enough to create a permanent middle class.

The pyramid of human society is itself undergoing a transition as the world progresses and the middle class can be no more than a stage during this transition. Capitalism has a mind of it's own and when the postwar years with America the only advanced country that was anything like fully intact, brought an opportunity to greatly expand the economy. But the commoner working class would not have had the money for tuition and capital.

The capitalism and democracy system took care of that, the government helped with the G.I. bill and supported or, at least tolerated the labor unions that demanded high wages. Unions began with the first merchant and craft guilds in free middle ages towns but the labor unions in the 1950s and 60s were part of the socialism borrowed by capitalism, which served as a vaccination against communism. Capitalism, with it's market forces did the rest.

The economy would drastically expand, it is today many times the size that it was in 1950. Technology would do fantastic things, such as landing men on the moon several times and creating the information superhighway. The communists would simply not be able to keep up. Postwar America to the turn of the millenium could be called "the age of the middle class". But now, it's mission accomplished and time to move on. The artificial middle class has served it's purpose well.

We could think of the postwar economy as one of the moon rockets that it made possible. It certainly took off like one. The huge rocket can obtain a high enough speed to escape earth's gravity only by the use of stages. When one stage has spent it's fuel, it is jettisoned, thus shedding it's weight. Holding onto the entire rocket structure during the climb would weigh down the spacecraft and with existing fuels would make the mission impossible. In the economy, that stage is the middle class, it is being shed.

The one hump of the dromedary is giving way to the two humps of the bactrian camel.

▼

CHAPTER SIX

CORPORATIONS AND OBSOLESCENCE

We reviewed the dynamic interplay between democracy and capitalism. The gilded age of capitalism was the pendulum far to the capitalist side. The postwar times of middle class and labor union and socialism in many other countries showed the pendulum to the democracy side. However, the explosive growth of corporations is bringing the pendulum back.

Today, the traditional idea of a nation is gradually giving way to the multi-national corporation as the holder of the real wealth and power in the world. If you would like to compare it to sports, the corporations are the teams or boxers, the national government is the referee and commission, it is the team that the people pay to see, not the referee or the sport's governing officials. The top one hundred economic entities in the world are about half divided between corporations and nations. Corporations such as

General Motors and Ford control more money than the vast majority of the world's nations, Microsoft is on about the same level as Ireland.

We could say that democracy has influenced capitalism in that the Rockefellers, Rothschilds and J.P. Morgan have been replaced by voting shareholders in large corporations. But the large corporations are increasingly the holders of money and the power it brings now. As formerly socialist industries in other countries are privatized, into the hands of private businessmen as in a purely capitalist economy, the shift of power and money from nations to corporations becomes even more rapid.

The automobile further accelerates and corporatizes a capitalist economy and, not just as an item of high-technology per se. When consumers drive instead of walk, their area of searching for the best deal is vastly increased. People no longer shop at a store just because it is the closest one. If a store is good, it will draw customers from far afield and gain the capital to expand. If it is not highly competitive, people with cars can much more easily go to other stores and it will go out of business even faster. It is also less convenient to stop while driving than walking and parking space is required. The consumer can also carry many more items in one shopping trip. This effectively puts most small shops out of business in favor of large stores and malls, where most of the tenants are franchises rather than traditional small, locally owned shops. Also, with all the moving in our society, people like to shop and eat at familiar places with standardized quality.

This means that the effect of the automobile is corporatization, the elimination of traditional small, locally owned shops in favor of large corporations, which may be international. Thanks in large part to the automobile, it is the large corporation that is gaining control of the world economy.

The computer accelerates and corporatizes the economy in another way, standardization. Henry Ford's assembly line became famous for reaping the benefits of standardization,. But, it is computers, more than any other consumer and business item, that depends on widely accepted standards, and not only in the use of the qwerty keyboard design. If one computer is even a little more popular than another one, software companies would rather write software for it and it can lower it's cost relative to it's competitor and become even more popular. This occured when IBM computers overtook Tandys and Macs. Giant IBM's domination of computer manufacturing in America promoted widespread standardization, unlike in Europe where many small computer makers produced incompatible hardware systems. This means that there will be no long drawn out competition, a small number of companies will gain domination in a short time.

What this shift of power to the corporations that is today's version of the gilded age of capitalism means to us is simple. The mission of a democratic nation is to look out for the welfare of it's citizens. The mission of a company, whether led by one powerful man in the gilded age or by a board of directors today, is to make money. A worker in a democracy is a citizen with the same rights as everyone else. A worker in a company is easily expendable unless they are an elite with high value to the company.

The pyramid of human society is going back to it's historic structure following the temporary stage of the middle class, with a few on the top and the many down below.

There are far more Americans on the top than formerly and fewer below, but this has been balanced by the millions of foreign laborers that are effectively working for Americans, whether or not they are offshore. This internationalization is not a fundamental change in the nature of the pyramid itself, but it does mean that the pyramid of American economic society is merging with the larger pyramid of the world economy, at the same time that other countries merge their pyramids too.

Along with them on the lower level of the pyramid are those American families that did not go high enough on the upward climb to get into the upper hump which makes up the top of the pyramid. Like an opening in traffic, the middle class was a chance to get into a lane moving ahead faster, but the opening is not lasting indefinitely.

Americans like to denounce the socialism in other countries as artificial according to the rules of capitalism. But the large middle class in America falls into the same category. Both of them have served their purposes well and are on their way out. Fortunately, these two concepts are not as large or as nebulous as the stock and real estate markets so, there will not be a sudden bubble burst. But the steady decline has been underway for years in both world socialism and the American middle class.

OBSOLESCENCE

The meaning of all this for the economy and everyone participating in it is very simple. Decent paying positions for commoner jobs are drying up, positions for elites are generally increasing. This is a basic shift in the nature of the human pyramid, not just a temporary change in the position of the capitalist pendulum. The children of a laborer have a much slimmer chance of finding a well-paying factory or other commoner job. If manufacturing followed agriculture in the sequence of economic revolutions in human history, and now only about two percent of Americans work in agriculture, why should manufacturing not follow a similar pattern?

The combination of labor and skill are what a worker has to offer in exchange for a living. But, labor is getting to be much more available relative to the skills needed in the marketplace. And you know what the law of supply and demand has to say about that. There are just too many people, young and old, who would like to happen across a high-wage, low-skill job. Also, do not forget that for the simple commoner tasks, there will always be an army of students working their way through college.

The worst case scenario is cruel, sudden obsolescence. We are taught that each of us is special as a person and we are, but not in the world economy we aren't. It is a throwback to the predator and prey relationship in nature that capitalism so resembles. It is the price to pay for an efficient, high-tech economy that can give us a better life. In this case, it is dividing the workers into those who can outwit and outrun obsolescence and those who cannot.

It is almost like a stock market bubble bursting. During the Reagan and Thatcher years, it was one group after another in the news; American farmers, Welsh coal miners, American steel workers. That does not mean that elites are spared; especially in professions like aerospace, defense and, military officers. But elites usually have skills that are transferable, and they usually get eliminated by attrition or, at least with a golden parachute, while commoners get the standard pink slip.

Commoners as we know them deserve credit for playing a monumental role in building the world from the industrial revolution until now. But scribes and blacksmiths, serfs and morse code operators deserve credit too. Commoners belong with them, holding a very special place. But they belong in the history books, rather than in daily life.

Reaching the era of the information superhighway can be compared to a drive across time. New positions are always coming into view as old positions fade from view. Some trucks and cars from other regions and nations are not going as fast as us and lag behind, seeing scenery that we already saw. A great mountain of factory workers has been alongside us for quite some time, but now it is fading into the rear view mirror. We can see that we are passing from one kind of terrain into another, even if the road is not perfectly straight and sometimes does not go between two points by the quickest possible route. But we can clearly see the future terrain coming into view while that of the past is fading. We have a pretty good idea what is up ahead but do not know for sure. There are speculations but no accurate maps. We assume that the road will continue straight ahead, but we can only guess at that too. The only thing we do know for sure is that we will not be seeing the scenery that we have past again, except in the photographs we took and memories.

WARNING SIGNS

There is little doubt that this primal shift is happening in the economy now. So, you should be able to see various warning signs all around you that times are changing.

All you have to do is look at the technology in use today, that should be warning in itself. The work force not only has to adapt to using this technology, but also to designing and maintaining it and, especially to producing it.

Read the employment section of a large city newspaper, not just the want ads but, the entire employment section which usually comes out in the Sunday edition. What kind of jobs do you see, commoner or elite? Look in any projection of future employment trends, which ones predominate, commoner or elite?

One thing that you have no doubt seen a lot of, depending on where you live, is empty buildings. This may not seem like an immediate warning sign, depending on what kind of building it is. What these buildings stand for is the obsolescence factor in a capitalist economy. You see buildings that once housed stores or other enterprises with "for sale" or, "for rent" signs out in front, or entire former shopping malls converted to other uses.

A lot of planning went into those buildings and they once aroused high hopes at their grand openings and the buildings look like they should be good for another thirty or forty years. What happened? Capitalist obsolescence is what happened. This is certainly the wasteful side of capitalism, but it is a system that is mercilessly efficient and with no tolerance for the obsolete. Unfortunately, obsolescence did not end with the ghost towns of the old west, left with no reason to exist once the gold was mined out. The only alternative for people is to adapt and improve, which is what has made capitalism so efficient.

Unemployment statistics can be deceptive. They tell you how many people have jobs and how many do not.

But they do not portray under-employment. That is, the many people who are working but, not at their true capability and potential.

Even though an entire region of America is now called the "rust belt", industrial areas of towns and cities can also be very visually deceptive. If you drive through a local industrial district, you may still see most of the plants that were there during the 1950's and 60's, some of them may have even expanded since then. You may very well see some newer plants too.

But what you cannot see from outside is that plants that may once have had 300-400 employees now may have only 60-70. And unlike in days past, many of them have to also have their wives working to make ends meet. Commoner laborers needing their wives working in large numbers was one of the early signs of changing times for the middle class.

Traditional large industries are downsizing as technology advances and branches out, but this is producing a multitude of small, more modern firms and in the new industrial parks, the new economy can be seen growing as a wide variety of high-tech, computer and, biotech firms. If you want to compare it to climbing a tree, we are past the trunk, the large traditional industries, and into a multitude of higher branches, which will in turn branch out into a multitude of still higher branches.

Anyone who has been around a while can see how difficult it has gotten to find good-paying commoner jobs. And layoffs in such jobs seem much more likely to be permanent than they used to be. There are fewer strikes simply because they cannot be gotten away with. Fewer demands for higher wages because the workers feel lucky to have a job at all. There are advertisements for laborers, but usually only as temporaries.

You see older people working as clerks at convenience stores and as security guards, having lost the jobs they once imagined would be secure for life. Many more older people are trying to fit in back at college, which is to be commended but is also a sign that things are changing. You probably know quite a few of them.

If you live in an industrial town where there is one area that is more prosperous than another, you will probably see a number of grown children of commoners who grew up in the prosperous area, got jobs in the same economic class as their parents, but who now own homes in the less prosperous area.

When you read the newspaper, there will be stories of international trade agreements such as between nations of the western hemisphere. There are the "maquiladoras" in Mexico's border areas, where American companies build factories to take advantage of lower wages there. There are stories from huge workshops in the third world of workers willing to work for less than a dollar a day for western companies doing assembly tasks. Many upheavals in American industries come about because the work can be done far cheaper overseas. American consumers complain about the lack of the high-wage, low-skill jobs that there used to be but, they certainly do not complain about the lower prices made possible by having the labor done overseas.

Likewise with illegal immigrants in the United States. A lot of people want to put more effort into rounding them up and sending them home, feeling that they are a drain on taxpayers. But when these people eat in a restaurant using illegal immigrants as cooks and dishwashers, they do not seem to mind the lower prices made possible by their use. If the resturanteur had to pay standard wages and benefits to those workers, prices in the restaurant may have to be considerably higher.

According to capitalist principles, the borders between nations are highly artificial. Just as the middle class and socialism were merely stages along the way, national economies are only a stage on the way to a global economy. Products and money freely cross borders, why not workers as they already do between western European nations? American farms make wide use of foreign migrant laborers, many businesses quietly use illegal aliens to stay competitive, American manufacturers send millions of worker-hours of tasks overseas, the trend can only increase. After all, as much as American consumers complain about the lack of high-wage, low-skill jobs, they never complain about lower prices.

As a final warning, just look at what the times we live in are being called. The shift in the human pyramid that we discussed is usually referred to as the "communications revolution". Every era is given some kind of name. Ours is usually called the "information age", the "space age" or occasionally, the "plastics age". Ominously, it is also known as the "post-industrial age". But whatever it's name is, I have never heard it called the "laborer age", the "tradesman age" or the "industrial age". Whatever you want to call the age we live in, one of the new words it has contributed to the English language is "downsizing", but you probably do not need to have that defined.

There used to be a time around 1900 or so, that the few elites were actually known as the "leisure class" because there was so little for them to do. But to the many commoners of the time, a 12- or 14-hour day was not unusual. The situation has become almost a mirror image reversal since then. This shows as clearly as anything the direction the world is moving, except that the commoners will become the "minimum wage class" instead of the leisure class.

The terms "elite" and "commoner" can also be deceptive. An elite is not really "elite", they are in fact becoming very common. While commoners are becoming increasingly less common. It is just a choice of terms, you can even substitute your own terms.

FLUCTUATIONS

Just as seeing an industrial district in your town can be deceptive in determining the changes in the economy, the world is anything but a place where everything works smoothly and there are deceptive fluctuations in the curves of the decline of commoner positions and the increase of elite positions. If it were a world of perfect simplicity, the graphs would show straight lines or curves. But it is not and there are temporary dips and blips. A new plant may even open in your town offering many high-wage, low-skill jobs. However, it would be only a temporary fluctuation from the big picture.

It is not a perfect world and sometimes there is too many chiefs and not enough Indians. But more often, there is too many commoners and not enough elites. A fluctuation in the increase in the elite position was the great middle management layoffs of the early 1990's recession.

Different countries and different areas within the same country have different rates of change toward elitism.

But make no mistake, the curves of increase for the elites and obsolescence for the commoners are very clearly present.

CHAPTER SEVEN

▼

THE OUTSIDE WORLD

There is one vital factor affecting what happens to the economy that we have only touched on thus far, the outside world. Things would be much simpler if we had only our own country to consider, but that is definitely not the case.

Capitalism and internationalization go together like hand in glove. The world's borders mean much less today than they did in the past. Revolutions in communications and transportation can be considered as branches of the industrial revolution. Companies with large geographical markets could not have come about otherwise. Communications and information is now considered as a revolution all it's own. What these two major branches of the industrial revolution did was make the world seem like a much smaller place. You can now call virtually any telephone in the world from any other telephone, or e-mail any computer with a modem from any other. You can wake up in just about any country on earth and go to bed that night in just about any other country.

There are three major factors involved, each with it's own "point of view" on internationalization—democracy, capitalism and, technology.

Democracy is the one factor of the three that speaks against internationalization. If the government's job is to look out for the welfare of it's citizens, then maintaining traditional border controls will help them hold onto their jobs. In a democracy, a commoner whose job is vulnerable is just as much a citizen as an elite whose position is secure. But on the other hand, spreading democracy around the world requires a mood of internationalization.

Capitalism, the second factor, is all in favor of just erasing national borders if possible. A manufacturer seeking a market and laborers willing to work for the lowest wages cares no more about international borders than a consumer looking for the best product and the lowest price. Look at the products in your home and the myriad of countries in which they were made. Even such a thing as an "American" car may have parts made in a dozen different nations, not to mention those where the raw materials may have been mined. In capitalism, borders are even more artificial than the middle class or socialism, at least they served some kind of purpose as transition stages.

As far as technology, the third factor, it is what caused the borders between the world's nations to fade in the first place. The industrial revolution made it necessary to search the world for sources of raw materials and markets for finished products. As industrialism spread and became more important, it helped to start a cultural harmony across the world for the simple reason that a factory in one part of the world is just about the same as a factory anywhere else in the world. Now, the transportation and communication revolutions have made the world into a "global village" as it has been called. We could even compare the very idea of a nation state to the multitude of small feudal domains that existed prior to the industrial revolution and the vastly improved communications and transportation it brought.

It's no contest; considering democracy, capitalism and, technology as the major factors, the shift toward internationalization has far more in favor of it than resistance to it. Even with international political organizations like the United Nations, the G-7 and, the G-15, politics is far behind economics in internationalization. Any nation that tries to resist internationalization ends up suffering from being shut out of the global economy. This is not a pendulum effect that is going to shift back, either. Internationalization is a part of progress that we discussed as one of the four basic factors in chapter one. In seeking the peak of maximum efficiency of productivity and profits, it is necessary to look across the world, not merely within the borders of any one nation. The pyramid of human society in each nation is merging into a large pyramid representing the global economy.

ARTIFICIAL PROSPERITY

Artificial prosperity can exist in a capitalist economy, but only as a loan. Just as a loan is "artificial" wealth which must be paid back, the price to pay for the large middle class in America has come due. Labor unions and the many pay raises they secured for their members made wages very artificially high. And now that the economy has gone a long way toward globalizing, those workers are faced with an army of hundreds of millions of foreign laborers willing to do the same work for much less money. When the pyramid of each nation merges into a big international pyramid, that means that the relative position of any worker in his own country may be very different in the world pyramid relative to skill and wages. And as artificial borders are given less and less influence, the law of supply and demand will even things out.

Let's be honest, unions have made blue-collar wages very artificially high. The United States took advantage of it's position in the 1950's to build a middle class as a springboard. But a lot of that lead was spent on maintaining artificially high wages for millions of low-skill jobs. It was worth it to the national economy in the long run for those who took advantage of the springboard to move their families into higher, more valuable positions. However, as we know, not all of them did.

If America's blue-collar laborers still earned the pay that they got in the 1950's, there would not be the big gap now with the workers in the outside world. Yet if America's blue-collar wages had remained where they were in the 1950's, the middle class would not have been able to serve it's purpose as a springboard for millions to the kind of positions that would be needed in the future.

Commoner jobs have been artificially protected by national borders, in America and other advanced countries, in a way it is kind of the reverse of the iron curtain. There are hundreds of millions of hard workers willing to work for low wages in the outside world, quite a few of whom speak at least some English. What do you suppose would happen if tomorrow, all national borders were to cease to exist with respect to workers and wages, and anybody could seek a job for which they were qualified in any country and the law of supply and demand would settle the wages before long? The national borders of the advanced countries are a reverse of the iron curtain with regard to workers and wages and, it is just as artificial as the iron curtain.

The corporatization and fading of borders in the world can only mean favor to elites at the expense of commoners. It is commoners, rather than elites, who tend to oppose immigration. Not because they are a drain on social programs as in more socialist countries such as France, because per capita they are not. But because ambitious immigrants are a threat to jobs. To elites, internationalization means a larger pool of workers to choose from who are used to lower wages and a lower standard of living.

It is large corporations, run by elites that is bringing about the internationalization of the world. Not the small shops run by commoners. It is the cutting edge of the communications revolution, the domain of elites, that is turning the world into an ever-smaller "global village". Internationalization to an elite means a world of opportunities, to a commoner it means a world of workers willing to do his job at a fraction of his pay.

There are four great factors interplaying here; elite, commoner, machines and, foreign labor. Machines and foreign labor affect elites and commoners very differently. You see, elites are the only factor of the four that are indispensible. It is elites that conceive of enterprises that fill niches in the economy. The other three- commoners, machines and, foreign laborers are all interchangeable.

The elites need labor for their enterprises, but they have three choices from which to get that labor. According to the law of supply and demand, it makes no difference which one is chosen. In the advanced countries, the commoner is by far the most expensive of the three. It is only national borders that have protected the commoner and his bubble of artificially high wages thus far. The only way for the commoner to keep his position in the future is to drastically increase his skill level or accept drastically lower wages. The law of supply and demand says so.

THE SCOPE OF THE OUTSIDE WORLD

Most Americans have little idea how much their lives are affected by events across the world. The rise and fall of stock prices here caused by events overseas is only the most obvious. The places where the things you own have been made and the places where the raw materials were processed may well encompass a United Nations of countries. You probably have no idea how many services you use such as dealing with phone calls and processing forms are done outside the United States. America is the fourth largest nation in the world in geographical size but still, it is only between four and five percent of the world both in population and geographical size.

Almost all other countries can be divided into two groups. Those that are able to directly compete against America economically and those that are able to supply workers that will work for considerably less than American workers.

In the drive across time that we compared our move into the future with, it is inevitable that some of the other cars would catch up with us. The first category is basically western Europe, Japan and, Canada. Except for Canada, these countries were destroyed or badly damaged in world war two. As well as some of them going through the upheaval of giving up their empires as America was building it's comfortable middle class.

America's enviable position relative to these countries is what made the middle class possible. But now, America's middle class is on the way out just as socialism is in these countries, no more artificial prosperity or protection. These countries are able to compete with America.

If America manages to spread democracy and capitalism, the most efficient system, across the world as it is trying to, it will mean more consumers to buy products but also more countries able to compete with America. Also, when there is talk of trade agreements and the spreading of capitalism and democracy and the promise it has to create vast foreign markets and demand for American goods, there is usually a neglect to mention that the goods will probably be manufactured close to the consumption site rather than in America. Meaning more positions for the American elites in those industries, but none for laborers in America.

Western European countries and Japan have much less in the way of natural resources and geographical space than America. But this fits in perfectly with the emerging post-industrial society. The physical size of the buildings in the new economy is much smaller than the massive factory buildings of the smokestack industries, as well as making less or no pollution ot the air and water, ideal for Europe without America's vast wide-open spaces.

Also, high-technology industries use little in the way of natural resources, it is brainpower rather than resources that high technology relies on. Many countries have long realized this. Switzerland is a small country lacking resources and isolated by mountains, West Berlin as a city spent forty years isolated by the sorrounding East Germany, both had to rely on the manufacture of small high-precision instruments developed with brainpower and transportable by air.

The educational standards in at least half the world exceed those of America, in literacy and especially in numeracy. Although it is true that many students in other countries do not get the chance to fulfill their educational potential, it is also true that the governments in many other countries have more power to compel students to do well in school. Science, mathematics and multiple language education is sweeping the world while education in too much of the American system is said to be "dumbing down" so that everyone can pass.

On the bright side in America, having a big country that needed to be developed and that was the most capitalist country in the world gave the people a strong entrepreneurial spirit and tradition while European countries were having their entrepreneurial traditions suffocated by socialism. And Americans are certainly the most computer-literate in the world, Johnny may not be able to read or multiply but he can cruise the world on the internet. Perhaps a big part of the problem is that the large middle class in America and the socialism in other countries perpetuated the culture of the commoner and his lack of need for much education along with the millions of low-skill, high-wage jobs.

A primary issue for today's commoner is the hundreds of millions of foreigners who could take his place. Population growth rates in the developed countries such as the United States are nothing like those in the other countries which could produce millions of workers to compete with those in the United States, but which cannot compete in the same league as the United States because they do not have enough elites. The average age in Mexico for one is about eighteen while in America it is over thirty.

Imagine a fellow we will call Pedro. He is able to speak some English and would easily learn to speak it fluently if he had more chance to practice. Pedro is from a village in no particular country. He went to school but did not get the chance to go to college, although he did manage to get in some basic computer skills. Changes are coming to the country but not fast enough, the gap between rich and poor continues to be unbridgeable. Pedro's father was a small farmer whose life was a struggle, even though people in the village know how to enjoy life.Pedro operates a machine in a local factory, before that he used to work in a mine, the issue of organizing into a union has never even been raised, anyone considers himself lucky to make any kind of a decent living.

Pedro rents a small but attractive house, there is a beautiful girl who lives nearby that Pedro wants to marry, he only hopes to be able to provide her with a decent life. Pedro's brother has a young son who they all hope can move on to be an elite. Everyone in the village has heard a lot about America, they are just mystified why Americans do not make more of themselves when they have the chance. In the village, getting a chance to go to college or breaking out to move upward in any other way is a dream. The village has produced a couple of well-known soccer players but college seems the way to really be an elite for the village's children.

Pedro is one of millions of foreign laborers who would be delighted to take the place of America's commoners, in America or in an American factory in his homeland. Since a primary criteria in the issue of commoner and elite is whether the individual workers are easily replacable, and since internationalization is in full swing, the big question concerning any particular job is; Can Pedro do it?

Striking workers can set up a picket line to block replacement workers from taking their jobs, but in today's world, such a line around America's borders is not possible. However, it is far from just a question of how many foreign workers will be allowed into America. It is even more an issue of American factories, and those of other advanced countries, being located overseas. Lower transportation costs made possible the exports of entire factories as well as larger markets, especially now that socialism is on the way out across the world and there is little threat of factories being nationalized by the local government. The best-known are the maquiladoras in Mexico, near the American border. More television sets are assembled in Tijuana than anywhere else in the world.

Moving factories to other countries for the lower wages there is a matter of supply and demand competition. If one manufacturer does it, the competitors must do it to keep up. It is like competition between the European countries in the imperial age. Blue-collar workers may complain, but you usually do not hear people complaining about the lower prices that it makes possible. What would you do if you were a factory owner?

You know how merciless capitalism is with anything artificial sooner or later. Corrections inevitably happen, bubbles burst. Are Americans now being faced with a correction for having lived for so long beyond our means?

There is no supply and demand justification for the very high wages of blue collar labor in the United States, or the other advanced countries, relative to the outside world if American workers cannot do something that they cannot. An imaginary society of only elites would have difficulty functioning as would a society of only commoners. But commoners can be easily imported, while elites cannot without causing a damaging brain drain in their country of origin.

Let's go back to the general criteria that elites advance society while commoners maintain it. This means that while every country must have those necessary to maintain it, they do not need those who find the scientific and technical routes to progress, nor does it need those who start large companies. These things are national "luxuries". In other words, every country needs people who can build and maintain it's buildings and who can produce it's food and clothing or, at least something that can be traded for food and clothing, all tasks mostly employing commoners.

However it is not absolutely necessary for a given country to have many large companies, many engineers, research and development facilities or, scientific projects such as a space program. These things advance the world as a whole but basically can be done anywhere. If we are considering the effect on the world as a whole, it makes little difference where the microchip was invented or, whether a given large company is based in the United States or France or Brunei.

What this means is that every nation has it's builders, small entrepreneurs, laborers, mechanics, plumbers, electricians and, drivers because these positions are immediately necessary. But not every nation has the more advanced positions in any kind of abundance, the ones that move the world into the future but are not needed on a daily basis and therefore can be done anywhere in the world.

So, when the world shrinks into a global village as it has been doing for years, the commoners in the United States and the other advanced countries will find that every country has many workers that could do their jobs, most of them used to doing it for much lower wages. While the elites will not find their own counterparts to anything like the same extent, but will find a whole world of commoner laborers to choose from.

▼

CHAPTER EIGHT

Cultural Change Required

THE HUMAN CULTURE COMPONENT

Everything so far in this book is just review and background information. The politics and economics are only the stage, this is a book primarily about culture. Numerous warnings have been sounded and projections made that more elites and fewer commoners will be needed in the future. But very little has been said about the fact that a shift in the basic culture will be needed to bring this about with anything like the best efficiency.

Aside from the factors of the economic system in which we make our living that we reviewed in chapter one, there is another critical component, the one we call culture. Marketers take close account of local culture when advertising, yet while the projections show that we will need more elites, they usually do not address the cultural component in any depth. Considering the vast amount that has been written about adjusting to new technology, and the multitude of projections about jobs for elites in the future, it is incredible how little has been written about the necessary adjustment of culture to achieve the optimum ratio of elites and commoners. Democracy says that all citizens are equal and capitalism says they are not. But wherever the pendulum is between the two, culture is the sum total of everyone's attitudes.

We could say that there is a pendulum between culture and progress. The majority of the time, the pendulum is toward culture as there are no significant changes in the established way of life. When something comes along to change things, the pendulum swings toward progress. Then, as the change is absorbed into the culture, the pendulum swings back toward culture. This is how human cultures have built up over the centuries.

The capitalist system is brilliant, but like a computer it can only work with what we give it and, tell us what it needs. The rest is up to the human factor. No system is perfect, capitalism deals with products and producers, wages and consumers, but not with human beings. It operates on the human desire to profit and the fact that people will usually work harder for themselves than for someone else, it draws people into certain roles by market forces, but capitalism makes no effort to shape human nature beyond that. The basic capitalism-democracy system is already about as good as it gets, improvements from here on will have to come from the human side, whether it be in the character of politicians or the education and skills of the workforce.

We all want to be able to live better lives and have a more efficient society, but that means we have to make progress. Taking a step forward can mean the collapse of the familiar and comfortable. A few people wholeheartedly embrace change, many resist it and, the rest are somewhere in between. The idea of technology is to make life easier and it certainly does for those that adapt to it but to many people, the industrial era technology meant pollution and the post-industrial era technology means incomprehensible digital gadgets.

In the one floor up principle that we saw earlier, your floor is closing but the one above you is opening. The higher floor will be more efficient , but you may be quite fond of the lower floor. Unless you are undergoing obvious hardship on your floor, you may not want to move up.

In our rocket analogy with it's sections, some people might like the way the rocket looks with all it's stages. They may have bought a model of it to put on display. Just because the largest stage of the rocket is now obsolete, they may not want to get rid of it.

If we learn one thing from the twentieth century, it is that no form of statism really works. Communists tried to change human nature by changing the environment. It did not work because communism opposed human nature. Capitalism and democracy works much better because it takes the opposite approach, working with the fact that people want to profit and better themselves and, will work harder for themselves. So, that is where we should look to improve the environment, with the people in the system. The basic system itself is about as efficient as it is going to get for now. Progress is only limited by the nature of the people themselves.

Think of it as a truck behind a bus on a single-lane highway. The bus is going in the right direction but the truck could go much faster except that it cannot go faster than the bus. Because you see, the people in the bus make the goods in the truck.

CAPITALISM'S PEAK OF EFFICIENCY

Capitalism does have a certain wastefulness to it as we have seen in the form of obsolete buildings and workers that are incongruent with market forces. There is also a wastefulness to it from the other direction in the form of unfulfilled potential, the positions that could be filled but are not because there is no one available that is qualified. This should not be surprising, remember that capitalism is based above all on the peak pattern, the seeking of optimum efficiency. The purpose of the pendulum pattern is to continuously find this peak. When the optimum peak is found for any given point in time, there will be on either side of the peak, those components of the capitalist economy that are out of harmony with the system. Meaning that while the economy is at the peak of efficiency, it is not at the peak of potential. It is as good as it can get for now but is not what it could be.

Right now, on one side of the capitalist peak, you can see the many obsolete buildings and laborers that are out of harmony with the market forces. On the other side of the peak, you can see the elite positions that are as yet unfilled and, niches in the economy that are as yet unexploited because of a lack of qualified elites. In economic terms, that means those segments of the economy on either side of the peak that are non-functioning. These unproductive segments on either side of the peak of potential represent the gap between the economy's potential and reality at a particular point in time. Our economy and technology could do much more if it only had more elites.

Of course, we want to have the economy at it's peak of potential given what it has to work with, as well as it's peak of efficiency. The way to cure this falling short of potential in the economy is clearly to shift some of the obsolete workers to the other side of the peak to fill the unfilled positions. The only way to do this is to turn commoners into elites.

THE PEOPLE FACTOR

But the economy alone cannot make a commoner into an elite. An elite and a commoner are different beings. It is up to the people to become the elites that the economy is asking for. A capitalist economy can no more produce an elite than it can invent something or start a business. The economy can offer an opening and profit for an invention or a business, but cannot produce the invention or business itself, it takes a human mind and effort to do that. So it is with elites, the economy is offering positions and wages for them, but like inventions it cannot produce elites itself, it is up to the people to make themselves into elites.

We saw how capitalism, the most efficient system, could not have been implemented until society had progressed to a certain level. To have kept the more primitive system at that point would have been counterproductive. Yet that is what we are doing now, not economically but culturally, because we are definitely into a new era. Progress will inevitably bring new requirements from people as well as making established positions obsolete. There were times when scribes, blacksmiths, cowboys, pony express riders and, morse code operators were promising new positions opened up by a step into a more modern era.

Suppose you were an emperor building an ever-expanding empire starting from a single town. As opposition in the home area is overcome, you need only a few patrols in the area of the origional town. You want to free up men stationed in the home area to man the ever-widening front, because the more the empire grows, the more riches there will be for your people. If you were playing a game with toy soldiers, you would have no problem. But you are dealing with real people and, someone used to patroling in the home area would take some time to adjust to actually being at the front. There would be two separate cultures to deal with. So it is with commoners and elites in the ever-expanding communications revolution.

There has always been new positions opening up as old positions become obsolete due technical progress or geographic expansion. This has been going on as long as there has been human civilization and on a regular basis as long as there has been capitalism, since the industrial revolution. Capitalism is designed with built-in market forces to tell us what new positions are needed and which old ones are no longer needed. So why is there so much of a struggle to eliminate old positions and fill new positions now?

CAPITALISM IN THE NEW ERA

The reason for struggle now is that capitalism itself is in uncharted waters. Capitalism has handled the economy, it's changes and progress, since the industrial revolution well. But this is the first time that capitalism is functioning through a genuine economic revolution. Human civilization began with the agricultural revolution after the stone ages. The industrial revolution was the next change on the same scale. The industrial revolution, in which the central icon was the factory, included a branch dealing with improved communications which is now a revolution all it's own, the communications revolution. The present revolution is sometimes called the third wave or, the post-industrial era and encompasses all kinds of high technology. It's central icon is the computer.

Capitalism cannot handle the transition through this revolution by itself. Although it's market forces do point the way. This is a situation unprecedented in history in which the commoners at the bottom of the human pyramid are being shown by market forces that they must join the elites at the top of the pyramid by acquiring the requisite knowledge and skills. This is a fundamental change in the nature of the human pyramid itself, rather than a mere market fluctuation. Capitalism can only work with what we give it. We are being told through it's market forces that it needs elites instead of commoners, but capitalism itself cannot create elites out of thin air, we have to do that.

Culture is what we do and think as a group rather than individually. But a cultural society consists of individuals and change must come from the individuals. The move from commoner to elite must be done one person at a time.

A PRIMARY CULTURAL SHIFT

There has always been those at the top and those at the bottom of the human pyramid, the difference is that in past revolutions, both groups had to change, such as they did in the transition from feudalism to the industrial revolution. There were still two distinct groups, the few at the top and the many at the bottom, the familiar line on the human pyramid did not change, the serfs did not have to turn into lords. Also, the past economic revolutions took place slowly, usually over many generations. Now, within one generation or so, commoners or at least their children are being required to become what they know as elites, as well as coping with the technology and knowledge that the communications revolution is made of. It certainly requires a primary cultural shift.

Human society has always been made up of those at the top and those at the bottom and, the very idea of those at the bottom rising to the top has been culturally heretical up to this point. As much as anything in history, the line between commoner and elite has been written in stone. Up until now that is, in the communications revolution the old established divide between commoner and elite is no more than a shifting line in the sand. That is where capitalist market forces are at odds with the long entrenched culture. If we define culture as the things we use and the things we do then, capitalism's usual relationship with culture is manifested in the form of fashions in the things we use, but the relationship is a harmonious one. This upward shift in technology has called for a corresponding shift in the nature of the economy and it's workers, putting culture, regarding the things we do, at odds with capitalism.

Culture, especially a well-informed media culture created by the communications revolution, also has a pendulum element to it. In America, a cultural pendulum conveniently divides the times into decades, from even-numbered upheaval to odd-numbered settling down. The forties were the war and recovery afterward. The fifties were stable, placid postwar prosperity. The sixties were the upheaval of the Vietnam war, the counterculture with it's values change and, the civil rights movement and race riots. The seventies were a settling down after the sixties. The eighties were the modern version of the roaring 20's, a binge of gluttonous materialism. The nineties were another break to settle down between the even-numbered decades.

However, just as the pendulum pattern of a capitalist economy is not the same thing as a primal change in that economy, as the communications revolution is, the pendulum shifts that American culture undergoes every decade or so is not on the same level as the change that will be required to keep the capitalist economy at it's peak of potential as well as it's peak of efficiency. Many more elites and many fewer commoners are what is being called for. But since the entire history of human beings has had a few at the top of the pyramid over many at the bottom of the pyramid, which is the historical basis of the elites and commoners today, we should not be too surprised that we are having a cultural problem with the idea, and also with the effort it takes, for everyone to become one of the elites at the top, to completely change the entire long-established pyramid.

▼

CHAPTER NINE

CULTURE CHANGES SLOWLY

CULTURAL LAG

Cultural lag is the time it takes for the culture to catch up with what is really happening. This is only an issue because the world has changed faster than ingrained culture can adapt. Recent decades have seen the skill factor of the entire society greatly increased, fewer commoners who know more are required along with many more elites. But culture simply has not changed as fast. Slowly changing culture gives us a sense of tradition and identity but changes much slower than the market forces of the capitalism upon which our society is based. This never became much of an issue until relatively recent times.

The family is in unfamiliar territory in that for the first time in history, parents cannot teach their children all they need to know to cope with the world. The vehicle of continued commonerism is mainly the family, for generations, father followed son. Commoners were always considered as the vast majority and elites as special beings, this is changing but nothing like fast enough for the maximum progress of society. This is the first time that we all have to become elites. The familiar, historical line on the pyramid, at least in the advanced countries, is as obsolete as the commoner laborers in those countries.

The problem is that human knowledge and technology as well as world population went into a steep upward curve in the twentieth century while culture did not adjust as fast. All such changes in the past, including the industrial revolution, had been much more gradual. The rapid advance in technology has created a difference between market forces and ingrained culture. The two graphs, the increase of technology and the increase of worker skills, just do not match. We could take a group of infants from all walks of life and train them into the elites that the world needs most. But the real world does not work as well. The main reason for the difference is the commoner syndrome.

When you go from grade school to middle school, or middle school to high school or, high school to college, it is not just a higher level but a whole new culture. You would not want to go into high school with your personality still in grade school would you? It is the same thing with going from commoner to elite, a change in culture is required.

Fortunately, technological change affects only a segment of culture. It does not affect celebrations of a person's ethnic or racial background. It certainly does not affect religion per se, except that it makes it possible to communicate with a vast audience. But it does very much affect traditional ways of earning a living and how much education a person needs.

The issue of the outside world also has a cultural lag component. The world is always moving toward internationalism, borders mean much less than they did in the past. Another name for our times is "the global age" or "the international age". Americans, especially commoners, are legendary for their ignorance of the geography of the outside world. We have to realize that the 1950's were a unique time for America, it gave us much that was artificial such as the middle class. People who came of age during the 1950's when America was alone at the top of the world can have a very exaggerated idea of America's place in the world. There are probably hundreds of millions of workers who could replace the commoners in the advanced countries. Of course, the artificial middle class itself has been around long enough to become an ingrained part of the culture.

THE CULTURAL CREDIT CARD

We rarely stop to think about the fact that we want the latest digital technology but do not want the upheaval in the economy making millions of low-skill workers obsolete. We know that we have to accept this new technology and learn to use it, but we neglect the fact that we also have to learn to produce it. We have bought a lot of high technology with our cultural credit card, the payment is due and will keep gaining interest until paid. Of course, it is not you or me in particular that has to produce any given piece of technology, but if we do not learn skills with equivalent value to the economy while someone else is producing it, we fall behind and become obsolete.

When I was a child, my parents would sometimes make the remark toward an example of high technology or some great technical achievement ; "Isn't it incredible what 'they' can do". As I got older, I figured out what it meant. But at the time, it seemed as if we lived in a simple, ordinary town while out beyond the hills somewhere were people referred to as "they", who were able to accomplish all kinds of fantastic technical feats and knew how to make devices that would do just about anything. All of which "they" generously shared with "us", who of course had no idea how to make them.

I did not understand capitalism at the time but if I had, I would have had a lot of reason to worry. I would have known that according to the law of supply and demand, most of the wealth should rightfully belong to "them". While if "we" could not be bothered to learn how to keep up, or find a niche of our own, we deserved to earn lower wages and become obsolete. It would be only fair since "they" were producing much more of value to add to the economy than "us".

The fact that we also have to produce the things we use or something economically equivalent is nothing new, it is just that people only used to have to produce on a level with their own class, any position more advanced than that was the domain of elites. The complication is that now, there are no elites who produce high technology devices for the commoners anymore, we all have to become elites and be able to produce something equivalent or be obsolete. Elites have three choices to obtain the labor that they need; traditional commoners, foreign labor and, machines. Commoners are by far the most expensive and therefore the least viable. Their only option is to become elites, of which the economy needs more.

Traditional education has not prepared us for this, we are required to learn physics and chemistry but the facts are already provided for us in the textbook, we do not have to actually do research and find them ourselves. Education only has to be learned, high technology has to be conceived, designed, produced and learned.

We cannot have our cake and eat it too. We want the government to do all kinds of things but we do not want to pay taxes. We want a wide variety of products to choose from in nearby stores but we do not want hundreds of big trucks on the road. We want cellular phones and pagers but do not want the antenna towers in our communities. We want high technology but do not want the choice of learning the skills to produce it or something economically equivalent or being obsolete.

We have bought high technology with our cultural credit card and made it the central fixture of the economy in which we earn our livings, now each of us has to learn our share of how to produce it.

PARALLEL SYNDROMES

It would make it easier to understand the commoner syndrome if we examine it alongside other situations taking place in the world which parallel the commoner syndrome in that culture lags what is really happening and in doing so, prevents the maximum possible progress from taking place.

Guns have been part of American life since day one. In America's early days; independence had to be won, Indians had to be subdued, the confederacy had to be defeated, the west, where the law was often not well-established, had to be tamed and, wild animals had to be reduced in number. All pressing reasons for keeping guns around. But today, guns are not only no longer necessary but, cause America to have the highest murder rate by far in the advanced countries. A simple case of guns becoming a part of the culture, which has not adjusted to changing times in which guns in private ownership are no longer necessary.

Doctors have been warning for a long time how bad cigarettes, alcohol, lack of exercise and, certain foods are for health. The warnings are being heeded but it took decades for culture to catch up with what was known. Eating and drinking together was part of the culture and adjusting that to adhere to some doctors' warnings was going to take some time. We had to see a lot of evidence first.

Slaves in America were emancipated following the civil war. The law can be changed in a moment with the stroke of a pen but the culture cannot. Prejudice in the country as a whole changed very slowly and it is debatable whether the cultural reality of today has finally gotten around to matching the legal reality of 1865.

Women in the workforce became inevitable with the shortage of manpower in the second world war and the rapidly expanding economy afterward. This took a few decades to get used to even though it's economic necessity was obvious. This is also debatable whether culture has yet caught up in the way of equal pay for equal work.

In the outside world, culture is generally even slower to adjust than in the United States. When the iron curtain came down, it seemed like it would be a simple matter to implement democracy in the former Soviet bloc. But not so fast, everyone seemed to forget that Russia has had a strong leader for the past thousand years, there was no cultural basis for democracy and little tradition of entrepreneurship. Democracy has not been successfully implemented. Capitalism and democracy is obviously a superior system but, most people there are worse off than they were under communism.

All through human history, it has been a source of pride and security to have many children. And for most of that history, there was little reason to think otherwise. However in the twentieth century, advances in agriculture and medicine caused the world's population to explode. Look at a graph of world population against time, it's just incredible. We have been hearing for some time about overpopulation and how the world cannot keep going for much longer at this rate without some kind of catastrophe. Many countries would be nice places to live except that they have just too many people. But once again, do not forget about culture. Having many children has been favored throughout history and that is not going to change quickly, overpopulation or not.

India's caste system is an example of a hereditary, enforced human pyramid that is thousands of years old. The constitution of India today actually does not recognize the caste system, considering it as an outmoded roadblock to progress. But once again, an old, established part of the culture is not simply going to change at the stroke of a pen on a constitution. The caste system remains in practice, if not officially.

Most Asian cultures are known for their respect toward authority and emphasis on the group rather than the individual. Asian students in western countries are known to be well above the average. As we might expect, in recent decades the Asian countries have produced many thousands of brilliant elites in virtually all professions. But there is a drawback, a lack of inventiveness anything like the west. Asian elites have been very successful at learning what is known, but almost completely absent at genuine breakthroughs in adding to what is known in the last three hundred years or so. Japan has become famous for it's high quality cars, cameras, televisions and, other electronic products. Japan Airlines is supposed to be among the world's best. But Japan did not invent cars, airplanes, cameras or, electronics. Although the Japanese have made significant improvements to these inventions and have come up with new versions of western inventions, they nor any other Asian country have contributed any breakthrough inventions in the last three hundred years

When people have too much respect for things as they are, they may put a lot of emphasis on learning but are unlikely to come up with any breakthrough ideas to change things around. When people think too much alike, as brilliant as they may be, they are also unlikely to produce many breakthrough inventors who can see possibilities that the others do not. It takes some disdain for the way things are done to produce any kind of revolutionary or breakthrough ideas. It is nations like Britain and the United States, with the protestant think-for-yourself mentality and, where secular authority is not absolute that have been the most inventive. We have to wonder what the world would be like today if Asia produced breakthrough inventions at the same rate as the west since about 1700.

The automobile in America is a parallel to the commoner syndrome. When the automobile was first introduced, it was a rich man's toy. Even when it came into more widespread private use, it was still a luxury. But today, the automobile is a necessity in American life to anyone but those on the lowest economic rung. It has made the transition from luxury to necessity. When something that improves efficiency becomes widespread, it starts to be expected of people to have it, it ceases to be a luxury. The same can be said about elite-level skills and education, it was once an exception and a luxury to the great mass of commoners. But no more, being an elite with the skills and education is pretty much an expectation, not a luxury.

AMERICA

The United States of America was born in 1776. It came along at the right time to build itself around the industrial revolution and to profit from Europe's experiences in building a modern society. America attracted millions of immigrants to settle and develop it's vast spaces. The idea was that an immigrant could rise above his fixed station in life in his homeland and have the chance to be an elite in America, and that people working toward their dreams would develop the new land and make it into a great nation. Any kind of enforced class structure was rightly considered as un-American.

Certainly a grand idea but again, we cannot ignore culture. The immigrants who came to America were mostly from the lower classes in their homelands, their families probably having been in the class for many generations. It was inevitable that they would bring some of their commoner mentality with them. How much of that mentality would depend on how much of an immigrant they were as opposed to a refugee as well as their ages.

The ideal chance to get rid of a commoner mentality and replace it with an elite mentality is upon immigrating to a new land when everything else new is being learned. Some families did, but for others, few things work perfectly in the real world and this was one of them.

For one thing, America's economy was based on capitalism. This meant that an immigrant could start his own enterprise and determine his own destiny. But it also meant that the up and down cycles of capitalism would knock people's dreams down once in a while. To an immigrant who had recently been a commoner in a stratified society, this would encourage the dampening down of his dreams and maintaining the commoner mentality as a place to psychically withdrawal to during the down times. Also, a certain amount of homesickness is to be expected for most immigrants. Celebrating the old culture need not include the commoner mentality that they had there but it usually creeps in unconsciously.

Capitalism's turning of the worker into a mobile labor seeker is most efficient but it also makes it so that a substitute for moving upward is often simply moving. The worker remains a commoner albeit in a different country or a different region of the same country. Moving to or within a big country like America may satisfy the drive for upward mobility but it leaves the commoner still a commoner from a skill and education point of view. Also, in a big capitalist country where the most ambitious and enterprising workers are the ones that go where the best action is, what happens to the areas that are left? They inevitably become havens of the commoner mentality.

America's vast spaces have been a double-edged sword in another way. Farming, ranching and, mining are an ingrained part of the culture. An abundance of raw materials and good farm land made it so that America did not have to depend on the precision skills of high technology to the same extent that smaller advanced countries without these luxuries would have. But those high technology skills are just what is needed in the new economy of the communications revolution. America did not have to be an economy based mainly on brainpower and high-tech skills, until now that is.

FOR A LONG TIME

Commonerism and class structure was enforced in the past because stability of society was the main concern and also because of the possible need for a ready supply of soldiers. The long-standing social order showed little indication that it was ever going to change. Commoners, and their country cousins the agricultural peasants, lived simple lives with little education, knowing how to read and write was a luxury. After the industrial revolution, commoner workers each lived in their own little space in crowded cities.

Commoners had little choice but to be satisfied with their own limited space because there was no more room for them. They had the ability to be preoccupied with relatively trivial things because they had little chance of much education and no chance of ever being in the corridors of power, so there was not much need for an education. Also, unlike the "leisure class", most commoners worked very long hours and started work at a young age so there was not much time for learning beyond what was immediately practical. There was no openings for ambitious people anyway, there were more than enough elites to run society and large-scale business. Ambitious commoners were nothing but a threat to stability.

Just looking at those identical row homes that are found in many European cities every day is enough to turn anyone into a commoner even if they do have a certain coziness to them. Some countries became dangerously unstable, there were class battles across Europe in 1848. Britain remained stable only by exporting millions of immigrants to new English-speaking countries overseas. But the social order in the old countries was just not possible to alter. In the 1800's and early 1900's, there was nothing for millions of commoners to be except commoners. Since adoration of royalty is one of the most commoner of things, should we really be so surprised at the popularity of princess Diana?

Considering that one of the traits of a commoner is the ability to be preoccupied with trivial things instead of education and that the vast majority of us are of commoner heritage, should we really be surprised that television churns out hours of trivialities while childrens' educations are relatively neglected? Television may have been invented and developed by elites but most of it's content still reflects the commoner majority.

The idea that the average commoner could even dream of being an elite is confined to very recent times in a limited part of the world compared to the whole world and the entire history of civilization when it was almost impossible. By far the vast majority of people who have lived since the industrial revolution have been traditional commoners. Should we not expect some cultural resistance to the sudden change demanded by market forces?

In the animal kingdom, the young have always learned from their parents. Until the information age, humans had always been the same. This is the first time in history that society is advancing in knowledge and skill factor faster than the family and culture can comfortably adapt. While the change is inevitable and the faster, the better, we should not be surprised that things are not going as smoothly as they could.

If you study history, it is easy to see how the present is a product of the past. However, studying history can be deceptive. History is very top-heavy, you read proportionally far more about the elites and the heroes of the time than about the everyday commoners. But it is the relatively hidden multitude of commoners that the culture of any given time really consists of. This means that it is much less the great heroes that we learn about in school who have made society what it is today than the multitudes of commoners and the heritage they have left us.

CHAPTER TEN

——————▼——————

THE PERPETUATION
OF COMMONERISM

COMMONER HAVEN

A deep root of commonerism is bad economic times, caused to some extent by the cycles of capitalism's pendulum. It is much easier to be an elite when times are good and there is plenty of wealth to go around. For all the reasons to move to North America, it was inevitable that immigrants and, especially refugees would bring the commoner mentality with them, at least as a haven for those times when dreams did not materialize.

Psychology tells us about regressive behavior when things do not go our way. The commoner mentality is a haven for the whole culture. Britain is known for the Great Britain / little England syndrome. When things are going well, there is the "Great Britain" mentality when nothing seems to be impossible. For those times when things take a periodic downturn for one reason or another, the "little England" mentality is reserved as a retreat until things change again. When an entire class of people are consigned to being commoners, they often have little difficulty rationalizing it. In Quebec, elite positions used to be called "L'affairs d'anglais", the business of the English-speakers, to rationalize the fact that the Quebecois were effectively shut out of such positions.

In an area the size of the United States, the commoner mentality of course also has a geographic as well as a cultural haven. In a country where ambitious people move around in search of jobs and boom areas, those areas left behind will inevitably hold a concentration of the commoner mentality.

PACIFICATION OF COMMONERS

Before the massive expansion of the economy in the second half of the twentieth century, commoners were held down, there was simply nothing for them to be except commoners. Their potential brainpower or entrepreneurial energies were not needed. They had to be satisfied with their little place in the world, and so most of them were. Commonerism became deeply ingrained in the culture of western Europe and America, even though life was not very good in the gilded age of capitalism for a commoner.

One of the surest ways to sooner or later become an elite is to hate being a commoner. You would think that when the economy and knowledge exploded from the 1950's onward that people would be jumping at the chance to rise up from their low status, and millions of them were. But far too many of them were not. It turned out that maybe being a commoner was not so bad after all. Socialism, which served to make capitalism more viable, did so by making being a commoner more comfortable. With the improvements in working conditions, minimum wage laws, time and a half pay for overtime, labor unions bringing pay raises and, plenty of low-skill, high-wage jobs, life as a commoner did not seem so bad.

As we have seen, the middle class was both possible and necessary, at least at the time, and while it made it possible for commoners to become the needed elites, it also made being a commoner perhaps a little too comfortable for the long-term good. Those high-wage, low-skill jobs could not last forever.

In 1940, about two out of three Americans lived in a rented household. The great increase in home ownership since then placated the commoners, especially those remembering the depression. The typical commoner in the later half of the twentieth century had much more free time than formerly, it still was better to be an elite but at least those backbreaking sixteen hour days were a thing of the past, the unions would never allow it. The increasing lack of emphasis on dress also made being a commoner acceptable, elites did not advertise their higher status with top hats any more.

Another factor making life as a commoner more toler-able is that many commoner tasks, at least historically, are open to a satisfying hands-on craftsmanship that many elite tasks lack. Job satisfaction was an important element of many commoner lives. The advance of technology has meant that many commoners require considerable knowledge to do their daily work, making it intellectually satisfying. All of which improves life for the commoners and in doing so, perpetuates the commoner mentality in the long run.

THE LEGEND OF BILL'S FATHER

Commonerism has received it's share of glorification. I remember a story from when I was in high school in the 1970's, I cannot remember all the details or even the exact name but it went something like this:

A teenaged boy named Bill lived in a prosperous town and was in a class in school that was having a picnic by a nearby lake in which the students were to bring at least one of their parents, they were to go for a boat ride on the lake afterward. Bill's father, a mechanic, took an afternoon off and came straight from work. Bill had been looking forward to the picnic so that he could introduce his father to the other students at school. Unfortunately, things did not go as Bill had planned.

The other fathers were mostly professionals, all well-dressed, and talked a lot among each other. Bill noticed that his father was being somewhat ignored, he was not talking in the group with the other fathers. Bill and his father sat alone together and ate lunch on a picnic table. The day before, Bill and the other students had all been friends, now it seemed as if they were ignoring him as they introduced their fathers to the other students.

Bill had never even thought about this before, everything had seemed just fine up until now. Sitting alone together, Bill realized that his father was just a commoner and not in the same class as the other fathers. Bill wondered how this would affect his many prized friendships at school, all of a sudden it seemed that he was of a lower class than the other students. Bill could not wait for the afternoon to end. But then something happened to change the whole day around.

On the boat ride around the lake, Bill continued to sit with his father near the front of the boat. No one was talking to them, this was one of the most miserable days of Bill's life. Suddenly, out in the middle of the lake, the motor on the boat sputtered briefly and then went dead. Someone tried to restart it a couple of times to no avail. The talking stopped, no one seemed to know what to do. There was no way to call for help, the boat was drifting slowly but the nearest shore was far away.

Bill's father got up and said "let me take a look at it" he opened the motor up and looked at it for a minute or two while everyone watched, hopefully. Then Bill's father took out a multi-tool from his pocket, made a few adjustments, tried to start the motor, made a few more adjustments, tried to start it again and presto, the motor started and purred like a kitten. Bill's father returned to his seat next to Bill.

As far as Bill was concerned, the whole day was turned around, now his father was a hero. Those paper-pushing elite fathers had ignored Bill's father at the picnic but, when the motor stopped, none of them had a clue what to do. It was Bill's commoner father that had saved the day. And this was a day that Bill was never going to forget.

OPIATES OF THE COMMONER

Everyone has some desire to contribute to the world, to leave their imprint on it. An elite can naturally do it more effectively than a commoner, but there are enough ways for the commoners to feel that they are doing it to pacify them. Community activities can give a commoner a pacifying sense of contributing to the world. Family, voting, sports and, hobbies are other pillars of a satisfying commoner life.

Patriotism is often very strong in commoners. America has made folk heroes of those who labored on the Erie canal, the cross country railroads and, the Empire State Building. Except for architects, inventors and, some engineers, a commoner's labor is often more physically visible than that of elites. Prejudice is also a traditional opiate of commoners, not just for the threat to the commoner's job but to feel big about himself. I may not be an elite but at least I am American, white, Anglo, British, Aryan, etc

Commoner towns can be nice, cozy, communal places. If elites and commoners usually marry into their own group and commoners outnumber elites, that means that a commoner has a wider possibility of marriage partners to choose from. Love is another opiate, as a number of songs have pointed out. "I may not have riches but at least I have you". Surely, some of those commoner girls make being a commoner seem to be not so bad.

From working out to bowling and softball leagues to betting on sports to fixing up the house or the car, the commoner has all kinds of outlets for ambitions, although none of them will move him toward elitism. This is the way it has been since the industrial revolution.

Another factor today is that the commoner often has more time for family than elites or, if he works considerable overtime, may earn more than some elites. Staying a commoner has a like father, like son coziness to it.

Especially since being an elite often means moving to where the opportunity is.

Most women would probably rather marry an elite than a commoner. But that requires her to be smarter to keep up with him. Also, chances are that her father was a commoner and many commoner tasks have a macho image or an immediate practical application such as fixing up the house or taking care of the car. To a commoner girl, the world of elites may be unfamiliar territory.

In a close-knit community, someone too ambitious or successful threatens the esteem of others and the stability of the community. Tensions are inevitable when one friend or sibling succeeds and the other doesn't. It is a sense of shared struggle that does a lot to make the lives of commoners bearable. The same chance to show goodwill is not there for an elite who can afford charitable giving and not miss it. The depression years had a lasting influence in the bonding of shared struggle, combined with the fact that the elite robber barons crashed as hard as anyone in the depression. Coping with hardship has been glorified in popular culture, there is a certain rugged pride in making it through tough times. Something that only a commoner has. The Waltons just would not have been the same if they had been elites with a lot of money.

MACHO LABOR

The physical difficulty of many commoner tasks has significant appeal. When people talk about "work ethic", I do not think they are talking about pushing paper or pecking a keyboard. Commoners traditionally take pride in actual hands-on application of knowledge rather than book knowledge. And many of them of being tough, strong and not afraid to get dirty. The average commoner is probably stronger than the average elite, has more chance of having been a jock rather than a brain in school.

The explosion of knowledge and the economy from 1950 onward means that many elite positions are of relatively recent origin and so do not have the same cultural roots as traditional commoner positions. Combined with the physical difficulty or practicality around the house and car of the commoner positions, this has given blue-collar labor an aura of masculinity. Men have been mixing mortar, wearing uniforms and, tinkering with machines a lot longer than they have been using computers and working in most elite positions.

Culture takes it's time to grasp the fact that the elite is the way of the future and many elite positions seem wimpy or nerdy compared to those of the commoner. Foot soldiers and police patrolmen fall into the commoner domain and, commoners are more likely to try to be "tough guys" than elites as compensation for their lower intellectual position.

Were Rocky and Rambo from elite or commoner stock? What do you think? It is going to take popular culture a while to grasp the fact that high-technology is now a vital part of traditional "tough guy" positions. It still does not seem quite right that computers skills count for more than biceps.

Since it was in the 1970's in high school that I read the story of Bill at the class picnic, what do you suppose would have happened if the shark from Jaws had shown up while Bill, his commoner father and, the rest of the class were stuck out in the middle of the lake with a dead motor? There is no doubt that Bill's father would have gone into his Rambo mode and, while the elite fathers joined the girls in trembling with fear, would have made the shark into cat food and saved the day once more.

After all, Bill's father was a commoner. While those elite fathers spent their days in offices pushing paper around, he was out in the real world doing real work and, unfortunately for the shark, had a strength and toughness that they just did not have. Everyone in Bill's class would have taken a chunk of the shark home for their kittens and they all would have lived happily ever after.

Military service is a traditional source of pride for commoners. Even in the military there are ways to be an elite while remaining a commoner, as a member of elite combat forces or as a senior sergeant. Not only does the military have the most visible division between elite and commoner but is also an immense influence on culture. The army is the most commoner of the branches of the service and in almost all countries is the largest and so, the most influential on culture. The air force is generally the most elite but even there, the vast majority of it's members work at commoner tasks. The influence of the military on culture can only help perpetuate the commoner syndrome.

A modern volunteer military does not perpetuate the commoner syndrome as much because decent pay and treatment must be provided in order to attract recruits. This is more of a mirror of today's society than the traditional conscription military and the military forces in the advanced countries put continuous effort into staying on the cutting edge of technology. Even so, a military effect on culture can only act as momentum in maintaining the traditional views of commoner and elite.

AVOIDANCE OF ELITISM

There is probably just as many reasons to avoid elitism as there is to perpetuate commonerism. First and foremost, being an elite is not easy. You must learn difficult things, anything too easy to learn can never be the stuff of an elite, because then, too many people will be able to do it and it will not be as much in demand. Going to college or starting an elite enterprise requires time and money, the commoners around you may be unsupportive or unable to help. Being an effective elite means being a big, expansive person inside. There are exceptions to the home sweet home factor, but it is generally easier to be a commoner anywhere than it is to be an elite. One of the primary steps to money and power has always been to be where that money and power is.

Politics of any stripe almost always favors continuation of commonerism. Capitalism says that people are not equal but democracy says that they are. By allowing the commoner majority to shape policy by votes, democracy not only gives a commoner a sense of participation in the larger world but also perpetuates commonerism. Political revolutions in modern times have overwhelmingly focused on equality for all. The many plans for man-made utopias have tended to focus on redistribution of wealth to ease the lot of the commoners. Politics or not, being a commoner was always made more tolerable by simple numbers. It is only the fact that capitalism, rather than politics, is becoming the primary ideological force in the world that makes possible the economic obsolescence of the commoner in the advanced countries.

Labor unions have not only made being a commoner much more tolerable but also precipitated commoner bonding. Commoners going on strike and walking the picket line together was done in the same spirit as America declaring it's independence. The fact that commoners have associated mostly with other commoners has made it possible for commonerism to form a large sub-culture.

It has never been too difficult for a commoner to shift the world around in his own mind and minimize the things that he did not achieve or were beyond his grasp. One of the most frustrating and demoralizing experiences is to be a would-be elite among hardened commoners who do not want to spend much time talking about anything, such as high-level knowledge that they consider impractical. The would-be elite has little choice but to be one of them. Until relatively recent times, a commoner with too much ambition was considered as a dreamer or a threat to order and stability.

Being a commoner does not seem so bad when the troubles and responsibilities as well as the egos of some elites become known. It is easy to forget that there is a difference between being rich and being an elite just the same as there is a difference between being poor and being a commoner. The 1980's were not elitism but gluttonous materialism, a twisted example of not much more than the trappings without real elitism. The royalty, Kennedy and, Nixon scandals among many others have made it crystal clear that elites are human too. People in high places lie, cheat and, steal just like people down here.

Remember that elitism is an idea while elites are human beings, who were mostly commoners at one time, at least generationally. They occasionally exhibit commoner dispositions such as the building of glass ceilings. Richard Nixon was one example of a brilliant elite with strong commoner proclivity.

By it's very nature, elitism is bound to fail sometimes. Commoners and the majority of elites walk the trails that are already there. Elites advance the world, blaze new trails, and some of them inevitably turn into dead ends. Over the past couple of decades or so, the glorification of education has faded, clearly knowledge cannot solve all the world's problems. Even though the world needs more educated people than ever before.

In a complex, mixed-up world, who really wants to be an elite and have more say in running it? If elites run the world and the world is not perfect, that can only mean that elites make mistakes too. Stock market crashes, mismanagement of the Vietnam war, toxic waste dumps and, the challenger space shuttle disaster cannot be blamed on commoners.

Commoners are needed in a democracy, as well as in a capitalist economy, for such things as protesting ill-treatment of the environment and other elite excesses. There is a certain moral purity to commoners when discussing elites. Listen to factory workers talking about cold-hearted management decisions or blue-collar workers in a bar discussing the latest political scandal.

Having been a part of the culture for much longer, many commoner tasks have almost a spirituality about them that their elite counterparts lack. Occasionally, children of elites will fall back on commoner tasks as their own niches. You do hear of elites abandoning their careers to work at such things as carpentry or subsistence farming, especially in the sixties after nearly two decades of relentless postwar economic expansion. To cite an extreme example, we have the case of the unabomber.

CELEBRATION OF THE COMMONER

Many commoners are in a position to save the day and a lot of commoner tasks have high prestige. Firemen, mechanics and, plumbers are easy to forget until they are needed. The twentieth century has been the century of war and dictators as well as economic, scientific and, technical advances. This has served to glamorize the commoner foot soldier with his toughness and bravery preserving freedom. It has also been the century of skyscrapers and vast civil engineering projects all of which were actually built by the commoners.

Commoner laborers have their own holiday in the United States, labor day. But the greatest symbol of all of the commoner in the twentieth century was the communist hammer and sickle. Television has done much to make the lot of a commoner more bearable, have you ever tried to imagine how different the media might be if it was only intended for the elite minority? North America never went as far in glorifying the commoner as the socialist realism art from the Stalin era in the Soviet Union. But television has done a more realistic job of glamorizing the commoner. As far as I can remember, only Batman among our heroes came from the elite side of the tracks.

What about music? Especially rock music since it's birth and progress ran almost parallel to the vast increase in knowledge and the size of the economy in from the 1950's onward? Have you ever thought about how incredible it is that there are no popular songs about love of learning or, making a scientific discovery, inventing something or, starting a corporation? Even in a place like America where progress is the name of the game and the chance to move from commoner to elite is one of the primary reasons for wanting to be American?

Is "commoner rock" another powerful cultural force holding onto commonerism in defiance of progress and capitalist market forces? There is a smattering of songs about cars, partying and, drug trips and a few where the lyrics are unintelligible, the rest are about romance in various stages or one of it's aspects. There were a few songs in the sixties based on class affecting romance, one of the lovers being from the wrong side of the tracks. "Patches" by Dickie Lee and, "Down in the boondocks" by Billie Joe Royal were a couple of examples. Since then, not only has there never been a popular song about becoming an elite, I cannot recall any more that even call attention to the divide between commoner and elite.

It all, of course only makes being a commoner less noticable and more tolerable and contributes to perpetuating commonerism at a time when the economies of the advanced countries are demanding many more elites instead of commoners.

CHAPTER ELEVEN

▼

THE HIDDEN COMMONER SYNDROME

The insidious thing about being a commoner is that you can be one without truly realizing it. The commoner syndrome in America is in many ways a can't see the forest for the trees phenomenon. It does not get much attention simply because of it's lack of visibility. Throughout this book, I have used analogies and parallels to try to make visible something that is not readily visible except for the proverbial tip of the iceberg. There are many things aside from the commoner syndrome holding people back as individuals and society as a whole from reaching full potential. The difference is that the other things get at least some attention.

To begin with, the terms "elite" and "commoner" are themselves deceptive, elites are becoming more common while commoners are becoming less common. Class does not necessarily reflect character and the personal lives of

many elites are hardly elite while those of some commoners are very uncommon. I have just used these very general
terms simply for lack of better ones.

Nothing has hidden the commoner syndrome in
America like the middle class. It would be much easier to
see that there is one group at the top of the economy and,
another at the bottom and that we need many more at the
top and considerably fewer at the bottom if there were not
a big, comfortable, artificial bulge in the middle. Socialism
and the middle class improved the lives of commoners and
gave them the capital and free time to make an upward
move. However, in doing so it made it difficult for those
that did not move up to see the need to do so as the economy and knowledge advanced.

Television, as appropriate a symbol as any for the large
American postwar middle class, has not only glorified
commoners even as commoners were becoming economically obsolete. It has hidden the commoner syndrome by
giving us a much more visually oriented culture at the
same time that the differences between commoners and
elites were becoming less visible. In a culture where everything has to be advertised to get the public's attention, the
commoner syndrome is being inadvertently hidden.

We saw earlier that a drive through an industrial district
of a city will probably show that most of the plants that
were there in the 1950's and 60's are still there and some
may have even expanded. At least from the outside all
looks well, never mind that there is only a fifth as many
employees as there were in the plants' heyday. Television
over-emphasizes the visual sense and in doing so conditions us in a deceptive way.

In hiding trends such as the commoner syndrome, it is not only visually that the situation can be deceptive. A capitalist society produces a shortened sense of time. When short-term profit is what counts, longer-term concerns tend to get put on the back burner. Gradually, the culture at large has it's time concept shortened. It is no coincedence that Americans, historically the most capitalist people on earth also have the shortest time concept of any people. People in a capitalist society are used to the swings of the pendulum caused by the law of supply and demand but since this is a long-term issue of the pyramid of society itself, the commoner syndrome is not easily visible in the short term.

Industrialization also contributed to the shortening of the cultural concept of time. In agricultural societies, it is the calendar rather than the clock that is the primary measuring stick of time. A farmer does not have to plow, plant or, harvest at a certain time of day but he does have to do it at a certain time of year. People think more in terms of time of year instead of time of day, a long time concept predominates in agricultural societies.

But in an industrial society it is the clock, rather than the calendar, that is the primary measurement stick of time. A factory worker must punch the clock at a certain time of day and cannot leave until his relief on the next shift shows up at another appointed time. The time of day dictates events rather than the time of year. In a capitalist industrial society, a decidedly short concept of time is the order of the day.

Immigrants and their descendents kept the commoner mentality as a haven for when times were not so good. But what America is all about is success and times more often

than not are good. The commoner mentality was pre-
served, but put on the back burner. Once again, this
means that the commoner syndrome is kept out of sight in
yet another way.

One of the factors that keeps the commoner syndrome
so well hidden is simply the fact that it is difficuly to put
an exact definition on as well as having a relative lack of
visibility . The difference between other contrasting
groups such as blacks and whites, men and women in the
workplace, old and young, the handicapped and the non-
handicapped, the physically in shape and the physically
out of shape or, immigrants and native born Americans are
far more visible than commoners and elites. Numbers are
also an issue, in all of the above groups, the disadvantaged
group is a numerical minority. With commoners and
elites, the opposite is the case.

We hear about unemployment and occasionally under-
employment but, very rarely about underpotential, commoners who could have been elites. The political parties
are becoming more alike than is perceived, at the same
time as elite and commoner are perceived as less different
than they really are, even as the earnings gap between
commoners and elites is as wide as ever.

The brightest light thrown on the commoner syndrome
in America apart from the job situation is the outside
world. But even in the world as a whole, another visible
syndrome is overshadowing the commoner syndrome.
The historic desirability of large families is pushing the
world's resources to the limit and is not about to stop just
because improved medicine has dramatically decreased
infant mortality rates and have made large families more
of a burden than a blessing.

EXCEPTIONS

There are fluctuations in the curves on a graph of the increase of elite positions in the economy and the decline of commoner positions as well as many exceptions to the general patterns which can be deceptive, and help hide the commoner syndrome. Just as there is no precise definition of what is a commoner and elite but rather a gray area in between, the inevitable move toward elitism also has a few deceptive exceptions. Kind of like an ant walking across a wall of a certain color but with a few deceptive polka dots of a different color.

We have a success-oriented culture but, even more than that, we have a money-oriented culture. In fact, the gold rush-Las Vegas ideal is to get rich quick without working at all. The fact that there can be access to considerable riches without being an elite is the greatest blindfold to the existence of the commoner syndrome. It is possible for the commoner to come across riches even though it will not in itself make him into an elite.

The economy clogs up when too many elites or too many of the same type of elite is in a given area, just as it does when there are too many laborers looking for work, temporarily hiding the fact that the economy of the United States as a whole and especially the world as a whole needs many more elites. Our traditional view of class has been thrown off because many of today's immigrants are not poor and uneducated and do not start on the lowest rung of the ladder.

Each of these exceptions and deceptions each serve as another bush providing cover for the commoner syndrome.

THE PROGRESS DECEPTION

In the postwar years, much more brainpower and entrepreneurial energy was necessary for the economy and, many commoners in particular and all commoners as a whole have come a long way compared to their parents and grandparents. Women in the workforce have come a long way in the same time along a parallel track. Both were brought about by a mushrooming economy. But comparisons like these hide the fact that demand for women is not decreasing while demand for commoners is.

If all commoners were as commoner as they were in the past, it would be a national crisis. Fortunately they are not, many commoner tasks require skills and knowledge that few elites have. Unfortunately, this can be deceptive. If someone does better than their parents, they can assume that they are making the progress that is necessary to keep up with the advance of technology. When in fact, they may be nowhere near keeping pace.

What is so deceptive is that in America, where the difference between commoner and elite is not as readily visible as in other countries, is that the difference in pay between CEO's and laborers is the greatest in the world by far.

The theory is that as long as we just let capitalism and democracy work, good things will happen. The big advantage of it is that it does not try to politically manipulate the natural flow of things. But that is just what we do to our system except that we do it culturally instead of politically and we do not readily notice it because capitalism and democracy works the best of any political-economic system. We are human beings, not machines, and culture is a basic factor that must also be considered.

The down side of being in the lead or having the best way of doing things is that there is no one in front to serve as an example or a model for improvement. In the drive across time, America lacks a car that is well in front of us so that we can more clearly see what the future will require. When Sputnik became the first satellite in orbit, America had been shown up and realized it was behind, the reaction turned out to be one of the greatest booms for American science and technology ever. But now, we lack a nation well in front of us to make us aware of what could be and to spur us on to catch up.

STABLE HOMES

There are a multitude of other pressing issues that are holding back young people from reaching their fullest potential, as well as messing up their lives. These days, a child is considered as fortunate to have a stable home at all, regardless of whether it is a home with a commoner culture. Because a stable commoner home is a refuge in a world of broken homes, the commoner syndrome is neglected.

The commoner syndrome just gets hidden under drugs, violence, teen pregnancy, illiteracy, innumeracy, declining educational standards and, so on. The commoner syndrome is widespread but it is relatively mild compared with immediate threats to life and health. Even though I feel that it is a major contributor to all of the above. Commoners in the past had little need for much education and had little free time. Today, many commoner families have far from caught up with the need for emphasis on high-level education for students, who today have hours of free time. Too often, the gap is filled with negative and destructive things.

Another reason for the commoner syndrome remaining hidden is that while cultural lag is greater in small towns, the homes there may be more secure on average for a young person. Remember that the only reason the commoner syndrome is not worse than it is is that so many young commoners are locked away in prison. America has close to the highest imprisonment rate on earth. Few prisoners have the education and skills to gain a secure position in the economy if they were to be released.

INTENTIONALLY HIDING THE COMMONER SYNDROME

We have one group of people, the elites, who advance the progress the human race is making and cannot be easily replaced. We have another group, the commoners, that maintains the world and can each be easily replaced. According to capitalist market forces, we need more of the former and fewer of the latter. But by politics and culture we have smoothed over the difference between the two groups so that the demand of the market forces which would carry humanity forward is not being met as it should be.

It is still too easy for a commoner to minimize the importance of elite positions or convince himself that it is just not for him to do and pass the attitude on to his children, the way it has been for hundreds of years. We have made society more comfortable by painting over the commoner syndrome but, that is now working against us.

Many families used the large middle class as an opportunity to move up into the upper hump of the economy. But for those that did not, a disservice has been done by failing to call attention to the commoner syndrome, economic obsolescence could be the next warning for them that they are falling into the lower hump of the economy.

The intentional hiding of the commoner syndrome has it's roots in the necessary supression of commoners in days past. Until relatively recent times, there was simply nothing for millions of commoners to be except commoners. I read a story once about a boy in a commoner family growing up in Britain in the latter half of the nineteenth century. Tired of his grimy, industrial hometown of blocks of row houses, he decided to join the army and see some of the world since it was when the British Empire was near it's zenith. He made a life of the army as a sergeant, was decorated for his role in combat several times, saw more of the world than he ever thought he would, and finally retired from a satisfying career and bought a house on the same street where he had grown up, and ran a small shop.

Something just did not seem quite right about the story. The soldier had a glorious, satisfying career while serving his country and it's vast empire. But then, he wound up back on the same street where he had grown up. He did not rise up in the economy at all, regardless of how glorious his career, the places he had seen or, what he had done for his country. The soldier ultimately ended up in the same place economically speaking that he would have if the years he spent as a soldier had been spent at the local mill. In other words, he was a commoner and whatever he did, his place in society was fixed. There was nothing for him to be except a commoner whether as a soldier serving in exotic foreign lands or, as a laborer in Britain.

Today, there are still commoners in America and the other advanced countries. But they do not have to be commoners. In fact, they are needed as elites instead of commoners. Human knowledge and the size of the economy has skyrocketed, market forces are incessantly demanding more elites. The commoners' place in society is anything but fixed, the world needs far more elites rather than commoner laborers.

The trouble is that we still have not gotten over the cultural place of the commoners in their fixed positions.

The market works a lot like your body. Your body tells you what it needs and when it has had enough. Pain is to tell you that something is wrong. The way to good health is simply to pay attention to your body and give it what it needs. However, drugs can dull what the body is telling you and create artificial good feelings. The politics and culture that have countered the natural market forces are a lot like these drugs. The trouble with getting high is that sooner or later you must come down and may suffer long-term damage. So it is with the economy.

CULTURAL PENDULUM

What is very obvious is that we have to adjust culturally in order to use new technology. What is not so obvious is that we must also adjust culturally in order to produce the technology. We cannot keep having the latest digital technology while keeping the familiar culture we grew up with. The deception is that there is a much greater cultural lag for production than for usage. We must learn to use new technology immediately or it just sits there. But we do not have to adapt to producing it immediately as long as someone far away is making it. After learning to use new technology, there is no immediate reason to worry about our jobs or work skills or how different children's lives will have to be from ours in order to keep up with whoever is making it.

What is deceptive and further hides the commoner syndrome is that in a capitalist society, we get used to the swings of the pendulum of supply and demand but not primary issues of the pyramid of human society itself which are not going to change back. The advance of technology and the need for elites is a primary issue of the pyramid itself and is not going to swing back.

Belittling a commoner's life's work is not likely to be popular especially since we are now less class conscious and many commoner tasks are still obviously necessary and may require considerable skill. You do not hear much denigration of commoners any more such as a romance being threatened by one of the lovers being from the wrong side of the tracks.

Yet, it is clear that what is needed is for the pendulum to swing back toward glorifying the elites that the economy requires.

CHAPTER TWELVE

▼

THE COMMONER SYNDROME IN ACTION

It would seem to be a mystery why a country like America resisted communism as a political and economic entity while at the same time perpetuating commonerism as a cultural entity. The two have a lot in common. Both artificially hold people back from achieving the American dream and deny people motivation by preventing them from being all that they can be. Americans decry socialism, believing it to artificially protect certain sectors of the economy, but at long term expense.

Commonerism does the same, not politically of course, but culturally. To understand the commoner syndrome, it is vital to understand that it is the people that really count, economics and technology is just the stage.

Also, understanding the commoner syndrome would help with understanding of a wide range of human behavior.

Culture is possibly the most basic of the basic factors of a capitalist system that we discussed. In considering culture, it is the people rather than the market forces that count. We saw how anything artificial from a capitalist point of view inevitably undergoes a correction sooner or later. It is the same thing with culture. Workers caught in an unfortunate plant closing could be considered as victims of a cultural correction. The cultural time gap between learning to use and learning to produce new technology had closed before their work skills had adapted. Too many workplaces and careers today are artificial bubbles waiting to burst.

We know that workers caught in a plant closing is the most obvious example of the commoner syndrome at work. But if it is the people that count most of all then, we should take a closer look at it in the form of it's manifestation in personal behavior. Which is where the commoner syndrome really works.

THE COMMONER SYNDROME ON A PERSONAL LEVEL

Everyone is at least a semi-elite when young because their future is still open. A young person's realm of potential gradually closes as they get older, depending on the direction their life takes. It often takes until a person gets into their twenties and beyond for the commoner syndrome to reveal itself. How many times have you seen someone you knew after a long time and found that they have not grown any or expanded their horizons much since then or, maybe they have grown but you have not?

How many people did you grow up with that you feel could have reached a higher position than they did, but managed to reach a position on a level similar to their other family members? Have you ever met anyone later on that was a good student in school but you thought that they did not achieve the level that perhaps they could have? Even though there was no apparent destructive factors involved? Could this be said about you?

Could it be the commoner syndrome at work? For hundreds of years, a person's family, as well as the other families around them, which are very powerful influences, may have been commoner. The commoner culture in the family became firmly established and it is not simply going to change easily, even if the person is given the ability and opportunity to be more than a commoner. Family culture has just as much influence on a person as national culture, and as commoner culture is passed down from generation to generation it serves as a momentum preserving the past. Just as a train takes a long time to stop because of the momentum of the rolling stock.

When considering how much of a person's potential they have achieved, issues such as time, money, mishaps, choices available and, so on must be considered. Few people achieve close to their full life potential but, anything that holds a person back artificially from being all that they can be is probably commoner.

Being taught to be too easily satisfied is the mark of a commoner. It must be taken into account that a person's family background probably includes generations of commoner ancestors right up to their parents. As well as the great depression and other lean times when being easily satisfied with one's position in life was a bonus.

Unnecessary belittling of a person could be the ghost of commoners being forced to fit into their limited space in the world and, reminding their children and others around them that they had to do the same. Any kind of sabotaging a person to avoid being overshadowed is probably a commoner relic of the threat to esteem in commoner communities of anyone seeming to have more than their share. It would be less mysterious to those who analyze human behavior if these commoner roots were recognized.

Resistance to change is a hallmark of the commoner syndrome. A young person wishing to carry on the family tradition in a career must consider how that profession is being affected by changing times. One that wishes to continue living in the family's hometown should know that some areas get left out in a capitalist system and opportunity is much better in some areas than in others. And if a young person decides not to leave their hometown, that may only mean that their children will have to leave someday. The computer revolution may someday make it possible for anyone who wishes to be able to work from home but that day is not here yet, more computer elites are needed to work on it.

Awareness of the future and that times are changing is a mark of an elite. A person taking a job which may pay more but will not make use of training the worker may have or does not provide the learning or experience or is not a step on a career ladder or, lacks the elite potential of a job that pays a little less should really think twice.

Parents refusing to take an interest in their child's computer are doing neither themselves, their child or, their relationship with their child any good. This is one of the few times in history that the roles of the generations in learning is reversed. The way it looks at this point, computers are the future. Interest in computers is one of the most positive things a youngster can have.

Too much nonsense television is not modern, it is an electronic continuation of a commoner's traditional preoccupation with trivial things because they were denied any real involvement in the running of the world combined with the fact that commoners today have much more free time. The commoners' preoccupation with trivial things is the result of this limited role that they were allowed. A commoner is born with a mind the same as an elite but their limited role in the world means that commoner concerns and topics of conversation tend much more to the mundane and trivial than elites. Excessive interest in personal issues as opposed to real information is pure commoner. The perpetuation of commonerism explains the modern tabloid culture in print and on television.

The fact that we are in the information age and everyone needs to learn as much as possible is slow to become a part of commoner culture. Commoners historically filled their free time with inexpensive entertainment or socializing. The concept of using free time to learn and grow and become elites is alien. It is a testament to America's frontier and entrepreneurial traditions that so many former commoner families did manage to use the middle class as a springboard to become elites.

Anything that artificially limits a person from being all that they can be and contributing more to the world can probably be traced to the commoner syndrome, although this is rarely, if ever, mentioned. Psychology and the multitude of books analyzing why people act the way they do seem to completely ignore the commoner syndrome. People minimizing something that they do not have, or resenting someone who does have it, is often the cultural ghost of the closed and limited lives lived by commoners in times past, when an uneven distribution of the meager wealth was nothing more than a threat to esteem and stability in the community.

In the days of class systems there were different classes, one above the other but, those in the same class were perceived to be equals. No one in a commoner community was supposed to be above his peers, it was only a threat to esteem, order and, stability. The structure of the military hierarchy follows the same pattern, a corporal is equal to all other corporals. Influence between civilian life and the military probably flowed both ways. Today however, the concept of class must be dissolved to free the brainpower and entrepreneurial energies that the economy needs.

Traditions in some families such as the tendency not to show up the oldest sibling are other relics of the past, unviable in the new economy where everyone must strive to learn and adapt and, the levels of success and wealth that people attain will inevitably be far from even. When a person joins a group of people and feels pressured to give up legitimate interests in order to fit in, the source may well be the commoner syndrome. The essence of being an elite is to be all that you can be, while groups of commoners programmed to live in their limited space are threatened by any such expansiveness.

Artificial leveling of people in a group to preserve the group's coherence is more pure commonerism. The so-called crab bucket syndrome is possibly the ultimate example of the commoner syndrome. Crabs in a bucket together have been known to pull back down any one of their number that is on the verge of escaping from the bucket. The attitude between the crabs seems to be "If I cannot get out then you are not going to get out either". The thought that a crab which escapes may be able to help the others to escape does not seem to occur.

In the same way, artificial leveling makes commoner communities more comfortable. It never seems to occur to anyone that holding anyone back holds the whole community back in the long run. Commonerism often exists under the guise of community, giving little thought to how the children of the community are being hampered in gaining the skills and knowledge to cope with the world.

Pigeonholing is another relic of commoner days that has never died out. Every commoner used to have his own little space and his own "role" in the family or community aside from work. Pigeonholing people and acting puzzled or giving negative feedback when one shows interest in something out of his pigeonhole is pure commoner. Elites tend realistically to have many more categories to place people in, in contrast to the simple pigeonholing system used by commoners.

In days past, maybe this pigeonholing was more appropriate. Commoners worked long hours and had little time to develop multiple talents to the fullest, which did not matter much because there was little use for a wider variety of talents or knowledge anyway. However, pigeonholing in the information age is as obsolete as the steam engine, even though the producers of many of the television serials do not seem to realize it.

Suppose that there were two men in a commoner community, one was the "tough guy" and the other was the "smart guy". What if one day, the tough guy decided to start a reading program to really build up his knowledge? Or, what if the smart guy plunged into an exercise program to build a lot of strength? Depending on just how commoner the people were, negative feedback from the community would be the probable result. The idea of being all that you can be is nothing more than a threat to others' esteem in commoner communities. Not only that but, there would be little reason for a commoner to become educated, more elites simply were not needed. That is of course not true today, but culture just cannot change as fast as technology can progress or the economy can grow.

The story about Bill and his father is commoner in the extreme. It is at best an example of obsolete pigeonholing and compartmentalizing. How was it known that none of the elites would know what to do with a motor? Or that Bill's father, just because he was a mechanic would be a commoner? Maybe Bill's father could have used his knowledge of mechanics to invent and patent a new braking system, he could well have turned out to be the most elite of the elite fathers at the picnic.

On the other hand, maybe Bill's father might have written a best-seller on caring for cars or built an empire of auto repair shops. The story was just commoner propaganda. In these times when progress and change comes fast, a boy should be proud of his father without artificially glorifying the commoner professions and pigeonholing of his father's generation. Just as we can look to George

Washington as a hero without living the way people did in the 1700s.

The positive thinking and possibility thinking movements that thrived from about 1950 onward sold millions of books. The most famous author was Norman Vincent Peale. The movement conditioned people for success, for thinking of the possibilities that were within their grasp and believing that they could achieve them, while becoming better people and contributing to the world in the process.

What I do not ever recall any of the authors of the movement pointing out is that much of the positive and possibility thinking was typical elite while much of the negative, pettiness and, failure thinking was very commoner. After all, it is no coincidence that the movement got into full swing just as the economy was mushrooming after the second world war and the large middle class was opening up as a springboard for climbing higher. The positive thinking and possibility thinking movements made their millions by tapping into the need for multitudes of commoners to overcome the limitations of their background and become elites through the middle class.

Young commoners used to learn and grow until a certain age before going to work and marrying, which was fine since only a limited amount of book learning was of any use to a commoner anyway. Elites, in contrast, knew that a lifetime of growing and learning is necessary. Today, when things are very different, there is still a certain lack of understanding and unfamiliarity with the idea of people going back to college when older among historically commoner families. Once again, culture has not caught up to the changing need for elites and commoners.

This can also be seen in the marking of a person for life by school exams given at a young age that is still done in some countries. An accelerating economy and knowledge combined with a longer lifespan means that several major learning stages are becoming necessary during each person's life. While the culture as a whole is still having trouble getting used to people not having one job for life as they used to.

This age pigeonholing can also be seen in exercise. Sports used to be for the young, until it was known how beneficial exercise is for the not so young. Too many athletes stop working out at a certain age not as much because of lack of time as simply because that is the way it is done. Interestingly, I find that there are a far higher proportion of older elites in health clubs and gyms than older commoners. This should not be so surprising since we know that elites, unlike commoners, know they must keep learning and growing all their lives without being shackled by age pigeonholing, especially since lifespans will probably only get longer.

A wide gap in the attitudes of the typical commoner and typical elite is often seen in the attitudes toward foreigners. Commoners find it easier to feel threatened by ambitious immigrants here or laborers in foreign countries willing to do the same work for a fraction of the pay. A commoner may use prejudice against those of other races and countries to feel big about himself as a compensation for his limited position, while for commoner minorities, the reverse of prejudice is to blame prejudice for your failures.

Commoners have far less reason to be interested in anyone not like them. To elites however, foreigners and minorities are a potential market, a potential source of labor or, a rich source of knowledge. Elites tend to be better educated than commoners and therefore are more likely to know that stereotypes are often based on the least desirable members of a given group, that foreigners are not as different from us as we might suppose, that individuals are not responsible for the actions of their governments and, that inter-racial marriage is nothing new. A history book will show that people of different race and ethnicity have inevitably intermixed whenever they have found themselves brought into contact.

To see and understand the commoner syndrome, it must never be forgotten that hardly anyone today in the advanced countries is absolutely pure commoner. There is a sliding scale just as there is for political persuasion. Elites may still have traces of commonerism in them. A true elite will not have an ego about his position in the world since the basic definition of commoner and elite is their natural role in their order of things.

CHAPTER THIRTEEN

BECOMING ELITES

The industrial revolution set off a spiral of industrialization that put an end to feudalism. Capitalism emerged and promoted never-ending economic expansion and technical progress. Millions of laborers were drawn into urban factories and became the lower class while the factory owners became the upper class. This was a continuation of the familiar pyramid structure of commoners and elites, replacing the pre-industrial serfs and lords.

Industrialization vastly increased the scale of warfare, which promoted further advances. As the world recovered from the second world war, technology had progressed to the point where labor was becoming replaceable by machines and an incredible economic expansion was on the horizon as the communications revolution, which began as a branch of the industrial revolution, became predominant. But this would only be possible if far more brainpower and entrepreneurial energy was available to the economy.

The United States was the only advanced country not badly damaged in world war two. This created a massive demand for labor and a very high level of prosperity relative to the rest of the world as it became the focal point of the world's postwar advances. The result was a large suburban middle class in the 1950s where many people improved their station in life. Technical progress on all fronts, propelled by consumer demand as well as cold war military and space race requirements, could only be described as awesome. More and more brainpower and entrepreneurial energy was needed to keep everything going.

The glitch was that too many of the people could not keep up. Nothing like this expansion in knowledge, technology and, the economy had ever been seen before in history. Son had always followed father, but families found the world a different place when the children were grown. Education was easily available but something was missing.

What was happening was that we were still largely a nation of commoners thrown into the future. All this growth had just happened so fast and all the new technology was still pretty much a trapping to millions of people. The commoner syndrome gap became wider and wider. The positive and possibility thinking movements sold millions of books beginning around this time by tapping into the fact that multitudes of commoners needed help to become elites, although this seems to have never been mentioned.

As the other advanced countries recovered from the second world war and found new niches in the world after the end of imperialism, and industrialism spread to the third world, foreign labor became another critical issue confronting Americans. The days of the suburban middle class American laborer were dwindling faster than people could get used to the idea. It was not just a matter of learning how to use new technology as acquiring the skills to design and produce it. The alternative being to be worth much less in the economy than those that did have such work skills.

Capitalism was so efficient that communism simply was not able to keep up. Unfortunately, millions of workers in America and other advanced countries could not keep up either. Control of the economy was shifting from the nation to the corporation, many of which were multi-national and free to use less expensive foreign labor. Socialism had done it's job of making capitalism more livable and was on the decline around the world, putting the lives of the common laborers more and more in the hands of corporations, the primary concern of which is to earn money, not to guarantee the economic welfare of it's employees.

The expansion could go on until everyone on earth was working productively except that we are still far too much in a commoner culture. Things have moved so fast that the thinking of people is still in the patterns by which commoners have lived for centuries. As the expansion continues, many doors are opening while others are closing, it all depends on what kind of skills a person has.

EDUCATION

In an effort to keep up with the needs of the economy, there is much discussion about reforming the education system, getting back to core subjects, getting students more interested in school than television, budgeting more money to education, requiring teachers as well as students to pass basic competency tests and, so on.

But, I have yet to hear of educators really addressing the commoner syndrome or to see a book on the subject until this one.

A major part of the problem is that we are still too much a commoner culture. Considering that centuries of commoners needed little education to get through life, is it any wonder there is still a literacy problem? The trivial nonsense on television, which is a distraction to education, is a continuation of the commoners' affinity for trivial things.

It is a mystery why grades in school correlate so poorly with success in later life. Just as many intelligent and capable students from commoner families do not attain positions that they might have, many successful elites never graduated or, never went to college at all. Part of it can be explained by connections, available opportunities, early or late maturity, destructive habits or distractions and, the random ups and downs of life. However, I feel that is the commoner syndrome that explains the rest.

Every child has two parts to their education, the formal and the informal. The formal is an attempt to guide the student in the appropriate direction as viewed by society as a whole. The informal will pull the student toward family and the local culture. It is the informal that perpetuates the commoner syndrome. Just as overweight parents tend to have overweight children, commoner parents tend to have commoner children.

Not only are parents a model for their children but quite a bit of the actual education comes from them. Young people need a role model for their place in the world, not only for values. A primary criteria for separating commoners from elites is what if a person passed on their family culture to their children, would the children turn into commoners or elites?

A youngster can learn to be a good person while never learning to break out of the outmoded commoner mentality. Parents can tell their children repeatedly to get good grades but, there is more to it than that, the force of example is what counts. Can anyone deny that a child from a home with elite parents has more chance of going to college than the same child with commoner parents, even if the difference in earnings between the two homes was not great? Although as always, there are exceptions. An elite parent has wider intellectual interests and the child will inevitably be influenced by this.

Many things can make kids go astray or fall short of their potential and, we seldom stop to consider the commoner culture that they are growing up in. Especially in a time of drugs and broken families, a child is considered as fortunate to have a stable home at all, whether it is a commoner home or not.

However, the time for a child to become an elite is not in college but now, growing up in an elite home culture. A pressing reason to become an elite is to give your children the right environment to become elites themselves. And of course, not to become intellectually irrelevant to children that do succeed in becoming elites.

Anyone with a secure commoner position and not a long time from retirement may not need to be as concerned with becoming elite for themselves. But the issue is building an elite family culture for their children to grow up in. Because they will not have the luxury of earning a decent living in relatively low-skill jobs, like their parents or grandparents did.

Older people may have had to endure tough times in their lives. But what they needed to know to cope with the world is, on average, much less than it is today. Literacy used to be defined as the ability to read and write. Now it has been expanded to include computer skills and hope-fully one (or two or three) foreign languages. Not so long ago, it only required a high school diploma to be consid-ered as well educated. Now, an advanced degree is more like it.

Possibly the most important lesson to be learned in col-lege is to think like an elite. It is important for a student to learn about commoners, who have played an enormous role in the world, but that learning should be done as part of history class.

CHANGING TIMES

Thousands of years of precedent support the com-moner syndrome. However, there has never been a time when it has been easier or more necessary to change it. The cultural ghost of the class barrier is still there but, that is all it is, a ghost. This is only an issue if there is a doorway between commonerism and elitism, in a rigid class system, there could be no such thing as a commoner syndrome.

The fact that the commoner syndrome is largely hidden or, at least not as visible as other things holding people back from reaching their full potential, makes it more difficult to grasp but, once it is understood, it is easier to overcome. It is very fortunate that today's elitism is not a matter of manners, dress or, speech. When there is an ethnic or racial component to something like the commoner syndrome, it is much easier to understand but, more difficult to overcome. Fortunately, that is not the case now.

We live in a capitalist world with it's market forces. We are faced with a situation in which those market forces and an element of our culture are at odds. The only realistic option is cultural adjustment, one person at a time. It has to be understood that an elite is a different being from a commoner, when commoners try to join the elites, they usually only get the trappings along with an ego.

There can be pre-elite homes, where the parents have been commoners but are preparing their children to be elites. An ambition such as this may take more than one generation to achieve. An older person does not have to be an elite to help elitism along, just understanding it is a start. A primary difference between commoners and elites is that elites know that they must continue growing and learning for a lifetime, not stopping upon completion of their formal education.

The only practical way to end age-old inequalities is for everyone to become an elite. Many commoners are patriotic but there are few things better that one could do for their country than to become an elite and increase your country's level of skill. An elite culture is what will be needed by the country in the future while a commoner culture is a relic of the past.

In a similar way, to become an elite is to move your family and ethnic group up a notch. Some families which did not make it to being elites at the first generation in

America have another chance now. A person may have to leave their hometown to do so but, technology is shortening the miles with such things as e-mail. This is a chance to change the position in society that your family is in.

The overcoming of the commoner syndrome parallels the overcoming of racial prejudice. Not only are commoners not as visible as a racial minority, they are not a numerical minority. This makes the commoner syndrome not as obvious but easier to correct once it is grasped. Blacks have gone from slavery and sharecropping to being mayors of many of America's major cities. Think how much easier it will be for people going from being commoners to being elites, even though the commoners do not have nearly as much time to make their transition.

Women in the labor force are another parallel. There has not been a woman president in America yet, at least not officially, but women now head a number of major corporations. There was no alternative, much more brainpower and entrepreneurial energy was needed to drive the postwar economic expansion. As many people as possible had to be all that they could be.

There were many cultural digestions in the past which serve as precedents to the overcoming of the commoner syndrome. Any kind of revolution in economics and technology involving obsolescence of an old way and introduction of a new way brought the same thing. The families of blacksmiths and Morse code operators had to adjust when obsolescence came and, those of commoners today have to do the same thing. All technology was once new and alien.

The automobile is an ideal model of the change in the pyramid of human society. When the automobile first came into use, it was limited to a few elites. It gradually became more and more widespread until in the 1950s, most families had a car. The new suburbs that were built after the second world war were designed with the automobile in mind. Before we knew it, the car was no longer a luxury. It became a necessity as any working adult was pretty much expected to drive. So it is with elite knowledge and work skills, it is becoming a necessity rather than a luxury.

The original class system started with the upheaval of the industrial revolution. Those few that grasped and embraced it became the elites of the day, the families of those that did not became commoners. Now we are in the communications revolution and it will be no different. It does not mean that we have to throw away cherished ideas. We make a hero of George Washington but we do not still go to war with muskets, do we? The frontier days of the west are gone but, now we have the frontiers of information and technology, very different in form but no different in essence.

It took some effort and pressure but, millions of people have made health concern and exercise a part of their daily lives. Why cannot the same be done with the overcoming of the commoner syndrome? In the story about Bill's father, instead of strengthening the commoner position by glorifying what a commoner could do that the elites could not even though it was blatant pigeonholing, why not have Bill's father defeat the commoner syndrome instead of the shark by using his mechanical knowledge to patent an invention or write a bestseller on a mechanical topic.

The best way for a family to break out of commonerism is to use the changing times factor. It is often easier for immigrant children to achieve a higher level in society than their parents because they know that they have a different level of opportunity than their family has historically had. They do not believe that they are "better" than their parents, only that they have the opportunity to be elites that their parents never had. If their parents had had such opportunities, there is no question in the child's mind that they would have become elites. When commoners or their children do break into being elites, they are very often successful because of the hunger and the drive it took.

There is some degree of difficulty for children to achieve beyond what their parents did simply because parents are their chief role model and it has remained so for centuries. Unless of course, the children find themselves in a situation with much more opportunity than their parents had. Then it is to be expected that the children will reach a higher level. This is what should be emphasized to children, that they have much more opportunity than their parents had, as well as being required to have more knowledge.

Knowledge alone does not usually make a person into an elite but, it is the place to start for an upwardly mobile commoner. A commoner interested in high-level knowledge that may not seem of immediate practical benefit has taken the first step toward becoming an elite. Abe Lincoln supposedly would walk miles to go to school or borrow a book. A would-be elite should be aware of science, technology, foreign countries and, the global business situation.

The computer is only creating more positions for elites by widening the skills gap between commoners and elites. However, it can also be viewed as a tool for a commoner to work toward elitism as well as a boundless sourse of information. The best way to grasp the information age is to grasp it's central icon. The computer is an ideal central icon of the information age for another reason, it has progressed from the big main-frame computers understood by only a few elites to the PC, available to anyone as a key to the same information available to anyone else.

Unlike freedom, elitism cannot be fought for except against outmoded cultural chains. The greatest threat is human weaknesses; envy, jealousy, belittling, resentment of success. Some elites are known for their egos but as elitism becomes more widespread, there will be less and less reason for that. At one time anyone who could read and write was an elite but you do not have an ego today because you can read and write, simply because it is now the rule rather than the exception.

DOING GOOD

The first step in solving a problem or removing a hindrance is identifying and understanding it. That is the purpose of this book. The gap between economics and technology on one hand and culture and historical precedence on the other hand is a fundamental factor in how the world works in changing times such as these. It is not so much textbook history that counts in our case but the everyday reality that our commoner ancestors lived in.

I believe that a person has much more chance to do good as an elite. A good person can of course, be a commoner or an elite. But a good person living their life as an elite will have more opportunity to do good than one living as a commoner. This is not about wealth or consumption

at all, it is about bringing progress to the world and secur-
ing your own place and that of your family in the economy
at the same time.

When you or your children move up in the world, it
makes room for other people to move up too. With the
globalization of the economy, the more elites in the
advanced countries, the more chances for workers in the
third world to move up.

Science and technology have accomplished fantastic
things, including the conquest of diseases that were terrors
in the past. Just how much has been accomplished has
been offset somewhat by overpopulation. Science would
have already created a wonderful world if only there were
not so many people. Technology is fascinating, if you do
not think so, maybe you need to take another look at it.
Many great people put their lives into making it possible
for you to take so much knowledge and technology for
granted today. Much of the technology that can be seen
today is only just beginning to realize it's potential. Take e-
mail for example, it may make it possible for anyone to
work for anyone else from wherever they are anywhere in
the world. The more brainpower that technology had
working on it, the more it would be able to accomplish.

However, I do not want to pretend that knowledge and
technology is going to solve all the world's problems
because it is not. It can make a better tomorrow but
knowledge and technology are only tools, it is up to us
what we use them for. The human race has devoted much
of it's technical capacity to destroying each other, particularly in the twentieth century. But, that is a problem of
human nature, not of technology.

Being an elite on earth will give a person more of a chance to do good, but in itself will mean nothing when a person stands in front of God. After all, Jesus was a carpenter, a commoner. It is true however, that by becoming elites today, we are not being greedy but are only seeking to meet market demands. There is no contradiction in someone being a technophile and a Christian.

Religion is not the same thing as culture. Our culture is lagging behind economic and technical reality and in doing so, creating the commoner syndrome. Elements of our culture may be out of date but, culture is a changing thing, the word of God is not. I believe biblical standards and truth to be as relevant as ever even if the commoner mentality is outdated.

I believe that a Christian elite is the ideal person to get the millenium off to a good start. If you believe that we are now living in the times in which the biblical prophecies of the end of the world are falling into place, I also agree. But, it must be remembered that no one knows the exact time and Jesus did not tell us to stop living and making progress when it looks as if the time of his return is near.

ABOUT THE BOOK

In the early 1990s, the U.S. government set down the goal that American children would be number one in the world in mathematics and science by the year 2000. As of this writing, we have not come close to this goal but rather have slipped further. Reformation of the education system does not seem to be working in improving grades. Meanwhile, many high-tech industries cannot find enough workers with the required skills.

These are manifestations of the commoner syndrome. Many bright students fall victim to an invisible but powerful force holding them back. The first step to dealing with the commoner syndrome is to explore and understand it. That is the purpose of this book.

About The Author

Mark Meek is from a commoner immigrant family and has struggled with and, watched others struggle with, the commoner syndrome all his life. He decided that it should be nailed down and defeated. Mr. Meek is also the author of The Theory of Primes.

www.ingramcontent.com/pod-product-compliance
Lightning Source LLC
Chambersburg PA
CBHW031321290526
45784CB00014B/429